simple
low fat
step-by-step

THUNDER BAY
P·R·E·S·S

San Diego, California

Thunder Bay Press
An imprint of the Advantage Publishers Group
5880 Oberlin Drive, San Diego, CA 92121-4794
www.advantagebooksonline.com

ISBN 1-57145-742-9

Library of Congress Cataloging-in-Publication Data available upon request.

Printed in Korea.

1 2 3 4 5   06 05 04 03 02

ACKNOWLEDGMENTS

Authors: Catherine Atkinson, Juliet Barker, Gina Steer, Liz Martin, Vicki Smallwood, Carol Tennant, Mari Mererid Williams, and Simone Wright
Editorial Consultant: Gina Steer
Project Editor: Karen Fitzpatrick
Photography: Colin Bowling, Paul Forrester and Stephen Brayne
Home Economists and Stylists: Jacqueline Bellefontaine, Mandy Phipps, Vicki Smallwood and Penny Stephens
Design Team: Helen Courtney, Jennifer Bishop, Lucy Bradbury, and Chris Herbert

All props supplied by Barbara Stewart at Surfaces.

NOTE
Recipes using uncooked eggs should be avoided by infants, the elderly, pregnant women, and anyone with a compromised immune system.

Special thanks to everyone involved in this book, particularly Karen Fitzpatrick and Gina Steer.

CONTENTS

SOUPS & STARTERS

FISH

POULTRY

VEGETARIAN

VEGETABLES & SALADS

DESSERTS

CLEANLINESS IN THE KITCHEN

It is well worth remembering that many foods can carry some form of bacteria. In most cases, the worst it will lead to is a bout of food poisoning or gastroenteritis, although for certain groups this can be more serious—the risk can be reduced or eliminated by good food hygiene and proper cooking.

Do not buy food that is past its sell-by date, and do not consume any food that is past its use-by date. When buying food, use your eyes and nose. If the food looks tired, limp, or discolored, or it has a rank, acrid, or simply bad smell, do not buy or eat it under any circumstances.

Do take special care when preparing raw meat and fish. A separate chopping board should be used for each; wash the knife, board, and your hands thoroughly before handling or preparing any other food.

Regularly clean, defrost, and clear out the refrigerator or freezer—it is worth checking the packaging to see exactly how long each product is safe to freeze.

Avoid handling food if suffering from an upset stomach, as bacteria can be passed through food preparation.

Dishtowels must be washed and changed regularly. The best option is to use paper towels, which can be discarded after use. More durable cloths should be left to soak in bleach, then washed in the washing machine in hot water.

Keep your hands, cooking utensils, and food preparation surfaces clean, and do not allow pets to climb onto any work surfaces.

BUYING

Avoid bulk buying where possible, especially meat, poultry, fish, fruits, and vegetables. Fresh foods lose their nutritional value rapidly, so buying a little at a time minimizes loss of nutrients. It also eliminates a packed refrigerator, which reduces the effectiveness of the refrigeration process.

When buying prepackaged goods such as cream and yogurt, check that the packaging is intact and not damaged or pierced at all. Cans should not be dented, pierced, or rusty. Check the sell-by dates even for packages of dry ingredients such as flour and rice. Store fresh foods in the refrigerator as soon as possible; do not sore them in the car or the office.

When buying frozen foods, check that they are not heavily iced on the outside and the contents feel completely frozen. Make sure that the frozen foods have been stored in the freezer at the correct storage level and the temperature is below 0° F. Place in the freezer as soon as possible after purchase.

PREPARATION

Make sure that all work surfaces and utensils are clean and dry. Hygiene should be given priority at all times.

Separate chopping boards should be used for raw and cooked meats, fish, and vegetables. Currently, a variety of good-quality plastic boards come in various designs and colors. This makes differentiating easier, and the plastic has the added hygienic advantage of being washable at high temperatures in the dishwasher. If using the board for fish, first wash in cold water, then in hot to prevent odor. Also, remember that knives and utensils should always be thoroughly cleaned after use.

When cooking, be particularly careful to keep cooked and raw food separate to avoid any contamination. It is worth washing all fruits and vegetables regardless of whether they are going to be eaten raw or lightly cooked. This rule should apply even to prewashed herbs and salads.

Do not reheat food more than once. If using a microwave, always check that the food is piping hot all the way through. In theory, the food should reach 160° F, and needs to be cooked at that temperature for at least three minutes to ensure that all bacteria are killed.

All poultry must be thoroughly defrosted before using, including chicken and game hen. Remove the food to be defrosted from the freezer and place in a shallow dish to contain the juices. Leave the food in the refrigerator until it is completely defrosted. A 3-lb. whole chicken will take about 26–30 hours to defrost. To speed up the process, immerse the chicken in cold water. However, make sure that the water is changed regularly. When the joints can move freely and no ice crystals remain in the cavity, the bird is completely defrosted.

Once defrosted, remove the wrapper and pat the chicken dry. Place the chicken in a shallow dish, cover lightly, and store as close to the base of the refrigerator as possible. The chicken should be cooked as soon as possible.

Some foods can be cooked from frozen, including many prepackaged foods like soups, sauces, casseroles, and breads. Where applicable, follow the manufacturer's instructions.

Vegetables and fruits can also be cooked from frozen, but meats and fish should be defrosted first. The only time food can be refrozen is when the food has been thoroughly defrosted, then cooked. Once the food has cooled, then it can be frozen again. On such occasions, the food can only be stored for one month.

All poultry and game (except for duck) must be cooked thoroughly. When cooked, the juices will run clear on the thickest part of the bird—the best area to try is usually the thigh. Other meats, like ground beef and pork, should be cooked all the way through. Fish should turn opaque, be firm in texture, and break easily into large flakes.

When cooking leftovers, make sure they are reheated until piping hot, and that any sauce or soup reaches boiling point first.

STORING

REFRIGERATING AND FREEZING

Meat, poultry, fish, seafood, and dairy products should all be refrigerated. The temperature of the refrigerator should be between 34–41° F while the freezer temperature should not rise above 0° F.

To ensure the optimum refrigerator and freezer temperature, avoid leaving the door open for a long time. Try not to overstock the refrigerator, as this reduces the airflow inside and reduces its effectiveness in cooling the food.

When refrigerating cooked food, allow it to cool down quickly and completely before refrigerating. Hot food will raise the temperature of the refrigerator, and possibly affect or spoil other food stored inside.

Food within the refrigerator and freezer should always be covered. Raw and cooked food should be stored in separate parts of the refrigerator. Cooked food should be kept on the top shelves of the refrigerator, while raw meat, poultry, and fish should be placed on bottom shelves to avoid drips and cross-contamination. It is recommended that eggs should be refrigerated in order to maintain their freshness and shelf life.

Take care that frozen foods are not stored in the freezer for too long. Blanched vegetables can be stored for one month; beef, lamb, poultry, and pork for six months; and unblanched vegetables and fruits in syrup for a year. Oily fish and sausages should be stored for three months. Dairy products can last four to six months, while cakes and pastries should be kept in the freezer for three to six months.

HIGH-RISK FOODS

Certain foods may carry risks to people who are considered vulnerable, such as the elderly, the ill, pregnant women, babies, young infants, and those with a compromised immune system.

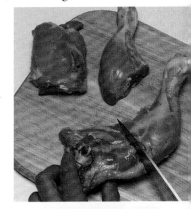

It is advisable to avoid those foods listed below which belong to the high-risk category.

There is a slight chance that some eggs carry the bacteria salmonella. To eliminate this risk, cook the eggs until both the yolk and the white are firm. Pay particular attention to dishes and products incorporating lightly cooked or raw eggs, which should be eliminated from the diet. Sauces such as hollandaise and mayonnaise, mousses, soufflés, and meringues all use raw or lightly cooked eggs, as do custard-based dishes, ice creams, and sorbets. These are all considered high-risk foods to the vulnerable groups mentioned above.

Certain meats and poultry also carry the potential risk of salmonella, and should be cooked thoroughly until the juices run clear and there is no pinkness left. Unpasteurized products such as milk, cheese (especially soft cheese), pâté, and meat (both raw and cooked) all have the potential risk of listeria and should be avoided.

When buying seafood, buy from a reputable source that has a high turnover to ensure freshness. Fish should have bright, clear eyes, shiny skin, and bright pink or red gills. The fish should feel stiff to the touch, with a slight smell of sea air and iodine. The flesh of fish steaks and fillets should be translucent, with no signs of discoloration. Mollusks, such as scallops, clams, and mussels, are sold fresh and are still alive. Avoid any that are open or do not close when tapped lightly. In the same way, univalves should withdraw back into their shells when lightly prodded. When choosing cephalopods, such as squid and octopus, they should have a firm flesh and pleasant sea smell.

As with all fish, care is required when freezing. It is imperative to check whether the fish has been frozen before. If it has been frozen, then it should not be frozen again under any circumstances.

NUTRITION
The Role of Essential Nutrients

A healthy and well-balanced diet is the body's primary energy source. In children, it constitutes the building blocks for future health, as well as providing lots of energy. In adults, it encourages self-healing and regeneration within the body. A well-balanced diet will provide the body with all the essential nutrients it needs. This can be achieved by eating a variety of foods, as demonstrated in the pyramid below.

FATS

PROTEINS

milk,	meat, fish,
yogurt,	poultry, eggs,
and cheese	nuts, and beans

FRUITS AND VEGETABLES

STARCHY CARBOHYDRATES
cereals, potatoes, bread, rice, and pasta

FATS

Fats fall into two categories: saturated and unsaturated fats. It is very important that a healthy balance is achieved within the diet. Fats are an essential part of the diet—they are a source of energy and provide essential fatty acids and fat-soluble vitamins. The right balance of fats should boost the body's immunity to infection and keep muscles, nerves, and arteries in good condition. Saturated fats are of animal origin and are hard when stored at room temperature. They can be found in dairy products, meat, eggs, margarines, and lard, as well as in manufactured products, such as pies, cookies, and cakes. A high intake of saturated fat over many years has been proven to increase the risk of heart disease and high blood cholesterol levels, and often leads to weight gain. The aim of a healthy diet is to keep the fat content low in the foods that we eat. Lowering the amount of saturated fat that we consume is very important, but this does not mean that it is good to consume lots of other types of fat.

There are two kinds of unsaturated fats: polyunsaturated fats and monounsaturated fats. Polyunsaturated fats include the following oils: safflower oil, soybean oil, corn oil, and sesame oil. Within the polyunsaturated group are omega oils. The omega-3 oils are of significant interest, because they have been found to be particularly beneficial to coronary health and can encourage brain growth and development. Omega-3 oils are derived from oily fish, such as salmon, mackerel, herring, and sardines. It is recommended that we should eat these types of fish at least once a week. However, for those who do not eat fish, liver oil supplements are available in most supermarkers and health stores. It is suggested that these supplements be taken on a daily basis. The most popular oils that are high in monounsaturated fats are olive oil, sunflower oil, and peanut oil. The Mediterranean diet, which is based on a diet high in monounsaturated fats, is recommended for heart health. Also, monounsaturated fats are known to help reduce the levels of LDL (unhealthy) cholesterol.

PROTEINS

Composed of amino acids (proteins' building bricks), proteins perform a wide variety of essential functions for the body including supplying energy and building and repairing tissues. Good sources of proteins are eggs, milk, yogurt, cheese, meat, fish, poultry, eggs, and nuts. (See the second level of the pyramid.) Some of these foods, however, contain saturated fats. To strike a nutritional balance, eat generous amounts of vegetable protein foods such as soy, beans, lentils, peas, and nuts.

FRUITS AND VEGETABLES

Not only are fruits and vegetables the most visually appealing foods, but they are extremely good for us, providing vitamins and minerals essential for growth, repair, and protection in the human body. Fruits and vegetables are low in calories and are responsible for regulating the body's metabolic processes and controlling the composition of its fluids and cells.

MINERALS

CALCIUM Important for healthy bones and teeth, nerve transmission, muscle contraction, blood clotting, and hormone function. Calcium promotes a healthy heart, improves skin, relieves aching muscles and bones, maintains the correct acid alkaline balance, and reduces menstrual cramps. Good sources are dairy products, small bones of small fish, nuts, beans, fortified white flour, breads, and leafy green vegetables.

CHROMIUM Part of the glucose tolerance factor, chromium balances blood sugar levels, helps to normalize hunger and reduce cravings, improves lifespan, helps protect DNA, and is essential for heart function. Good sources are brewer's yeast, whole-wheat bread, rye bread, oysters, potatoes, green bell peppers, butter, and parsnips.

IODINE Important for the manufacture of thyroid hormones and for normal development. Good sources of iodine are seafood, seaweed, milk, and dairy products.

IRON As a component of hemoglobin, iron carries oxygen around the body. It is vital for normal growth and development. Good sources are liver, red meat, fortified breakfast cereals, beans, leafy green vegetables, egg yolks, and cocoa.

MAGNESIUM Important for efficient functioning of metabolic enzymes and development of the skeleton. Magnesium promotes healthy muscles by helping them to relax and is therefore good for PMS. It is also important for heart muscles and the nervous system. Good sources are nuts, green vegetables, meat, cereals, milk, and yogurt.

PHOSPHORUS Forms and maintains bones and teeth, builds muscle tissue, helps maintain pH of the body, and aids metabolism and energy production. Phosphorus is present in almost all foods.

POTASSIUM Enables nutrients to move into cells while waste products move out; promotes healthy nerves and muscles; maintains fluid balance in the body; helps secretion of insulin for blood sugar control to produce constant energy; relaxes muscles; maintains heart functioning; and encourages proper waste elimination. Good sources are fruits, vegetables, milk, and bread.

SELENIUM Antioxidant properties help to protect against free radicals and carcinogens. Selenium reduces inflammation, stimulates the immune system to fight infections, promotes a healthy heart, and helps vitamin E's action. It is also required for the male reproductive system, and is needed for metabolism. Good sources are tuna, liver, kidney, meat, eggs, cereals, nuts, and dairy products.

SODIUM Important in helping to control body fluid and balance, and preventing dehydration. Sodium is involved in muscle and nerve function and helps move nutrients into cells. All foods are good sources; however, processed, pickled, and salted foods are rich in sodium.

ZINC Important for metabolism and the healing of wounds. It also aids one's ability to cope with stress, promotes a healthy nervous system and brain (especially in the growing fetus), aids bone and teeth formation, and is essential for constant energy. Good sources are liver, meat, beans, whole-grain cereals, nuts, and oysters.

VITAMINS

VITAMIN A Important for cell growth and developmemt and for the formation of visual pigments in the eye. Vitamin A comes in two forms: retinol and beta-carotenes. Retinol is found in liver, meat and meat products, and whole milk and dairy products. Beta-carotene is a powerul antioxidant and is found in red and yellow fruits and vegetables, such as carrots, mangoes, and apricots.

VITAMIN B1 Important in releasing energy from carboydrate-containing foods. Good sources are yeast and yeast products, bread, fortified breakfast cereals, and potatoes.

VITAMIN B2 Important for metabolism of proteins, fats, and carbohydrates to produce energy. Good sources are meat, yeast extracts, fortified breakfast cereals, and milk and dairy products.

VITAMIN B3 Required for the metabolism of food into energy production. Good sources are milk and dairy products, fortified breakfast cereals, beans, meat, poultry, and eggs.

VITAMIN B5 Important for the metabolism of food and energy production. All foods are good sources, but especially fortified breakfast cereals, whole-wheat bread, and dairy products.

VITAMIN B6 Important for metabolism of protein and fat. Vitamin B6 may also be involved with the regulation of sex hormones. Good sources are liver, fish, pork, soybeans, and peanuts.

VITAMIN B12 Important for the production of red blood cells and DNA. It is vital for growth and the nervous system. Good sources are meat, fish, eggs, poultry, and milk.

BIOTIN Important for metabolism of fatty acids. Good sources of biotin are liver, kidney, eggs, and nuts. Microorganisms in your stomach also manufacture biotin.

VITAMIN C Important for healing wounds and the formation of collagen, which keeps skin and bones strong. It is an important antioxidant. Good sources are fruits and vegetables.

VITAMIN D Important for absorption and handling of calcium to help build bone strength. Good sources are oily fish, eggs, whole milk and dairy products, margarine, and sufficient exposure to sunlight, which helps make vitamin D in the skin.

VITAMIN E Important as an antioxidant vitamin, helping to protect cell membranes from damage. Good sources are vegetable oils, margarine, seeds, nuts, and green vegetables.

FOLIC ACID Critical during pregnancy for the development of the brain and nerves. It is always essential for brain and nerve function, and is needed for utilizing protein and red blood cell formation. Good sources are whole-grain breads, fortified breakfast cereals, leafy green vegetables, and oranges.

VITAMIN K Important for controlling blood clotting. Good sources are cauliflower, brussels sprouts, lettuce, cabbage, beans, broccoli, peas, asparagus, potatoes, corn oil, tomatoes, and milk.

CARBOHYDRATES

Carbohydrates are an energy source and come in two forms: starch and sugar. Starch carbohydrates are also known as "complex carbohydrates" and they include all cereals, potatoes, breads, rice, and pasta. (See the fourth level of the pyramid). Eating whole grain varieties of these foods also provides fiber. Diets high in fiber are believed to be beneficial in helping to prevent bowel cancer and can also keep cholesterol down. High-fiber diets are also good for those concerned about weight gain. Fiber is bulky so fills the stomach, therefore reducing hunger pangs. Sugar carbohydrates which are also known as fast-release carbohydrates (because of the quick fix of energy they give to the body) include sugar and sugar-sweetened products such as jams and syrups. Milk provides lactose which is a milk sugar and fruits provide fructose which is a fruit sugar.

GUIDELINES FOR DIFFERENT AGE GROUPS

Good food plays such an important role in everyone's life. From infancy through adulthood, a healthy diet forms the body's foundation and building blocks, and teaches children healthy eating habits. Studies have shown that these eating habits stay with us into adulthood, helping us to maintain a healthier lifestyle as we grow older. This reduces the risk of disease and other medical problems.

Striking a healthy balance is important, and at certain stages in life, this balance may need to be adjusted to help our bodies cope. As babies and children, during pregnancy and in later life, our diet assists us in achieving optimal health. So, how do we go about achieving this?

We know that oily fish, for example, is advantageous to our health, as it is rich in omega-3 fatty acids, which have been linked with more efficient brain functioning and better memory. They can also help lower the risk of cancer and heart disease. But are there any other steps we can take to maximize health benefits through our diet?

BABIES AND YOUNG CHILDREN

Babies should not be given solids until they are at least six months old, then new tastes and textures can be introduced to their diets. Probably the easiest and cheapest way is to adapt the food that the rest of the family eats. Babies under the age of one should be given breast milk or formula milk. From the age of one to two, whole milk should be given, and from two to five low-fat milk can be given. From then on, nonfat milk can be introduced, if desired.

The first foods for babies under six months should be of a purée-like consistency, which is smooth and fairly liquid, therefore making it easy to swallow. This can be done using an electric blender or hand blender, or just by pushing foods through a sieve to remove any lumps. Remember, however, babies still need high levels of milk.

Babies over six months old should still be having puréed food, but the consistency of their diet can be made progressively lumpier. Around the ten-month mark, most babies are able to manage food cut up into small pieces.

So, what food groups do babies and small children need? Like adults, a high proportion of their diet should contain grains, such as cereal, pasta, bread, and rice. However, be careful, as babies and small children cannot cope with too much fiber in their diet.

Fresh fruits and vegetables should be introduced, as well as a balance of dairy and meat proteins, and only a small amount of fats and sweets. Research points out that delaying the introduction of foods that could cause allergies during the first year (such as cow's milk, wheat, eggs, cheese, yogurt, and nuts) can significantly reduce the risk of certain food allergies later on in life. Peanuts should never be given to children under five years old.

Seek a doctor's advice regarding babies and toddlers. Limit sugar in young children's diets, as sugar provides only empty calories. Use less-processed sugars (dark brown sugar is very sweet, so the amount used can be reduced) or incorporate less-refined alternatives, such as dried fruits, dates, rice syrup, or honey. Honey should not be given to infants under one year of age.

As in a low-fat diet, it is best to eliminate fried foods and avoid adding salt—especially for under one-year-olds and young infants. Instead, introduce herbs and gentle spices to make food appetizing. The more varied the tastes that children experience in their formative years, the wider the range of foods they will accept later in life.

PREGNANCY

During pregnancy, women are advised to take extra vitamin and mineral supplements. Pregnant women benefit from a healthy, balanced diet rich in fresh fruits and vegetables, and full of essential vitamins and minerals. Oily fish, such as salmon, not only give the body essential fats, but also provide high levels of calcium.

Certain food groups, however, hold risks during pregnancy. This section gives advice on everyday foods and those that should be avoided.

CHEESE

Pregnant women should avoid all soft mold-ripened cheese, such as Brie. If pregnant, do not eat cheese such as Parmesan or blue-veined cheese, such as stilton, as they carry the risk of listeria. It is fine for pregnant women to continue eating hard cheese like cheddar, as well as cottage cheese.

EGGS

There is a slight chance that some eggs will carry salmonella. Cooking eggs until both the yolk and white are firm will eliminate this risk. However, particular attention should be paid to dishes and products that incorporate lightly cooked or raw eggs, including homemade mayonnaise or similar sauces, mousses, soufflés, meringues, ice cream, and sorbets. Commercially produced products, such as mayonnaise, which are made with pasteurized eggs, may be eaten safely. If in doubt, play safe and avoid these products.

PRECOOKED MEALS AND READY-TO-EAT ITEMS

Previously cooked, then chilled meals are now widely available, but those from the deli counter can contain bacteria. Avoid prepackaged salads in dressings and other foods. Also, do not eat raw or partly cooked meats, pâté, unpasteurized milk, or dirty fruits and vegetables, as they can cause toxoplasmosis.

MEAT AND FISH

Certain meats and poultry carry the potential risk of salmonella and should be cooked thoroughly until the juices run clear and there is no pinkness left.

Pay particular attention when buying and cooking fish (especially shellfish). Buy only the freshest fish, which should smell salty but not strong or fishy.

Look for bright eyes and reject any with sunken eyes. The bodies should look fresh, plump, and shiny. Avoid any fish with dry, shriveled, or damp bodies.

It is also best to avoid any shellfish while pregnant, unless it is definitely fresh and cooked thoroughly. Shellfish also contain harmful bacteria and viruses.

LATER LIFE

So what about later on in life? As the body gets older, we can help stave off infection and illness through our diet. There is evidence to show that the immune system becomes weaker as we get older, which can increase the risk of suffering from cancer and other illnesses. Maintaining a diet rich in antioxidants, fresh fruits and vegetables, plant oils, and oily fish is especially beneficial in order to either prevent these illnesses or minimize their effects. As with all age groups, the body benefits from the five-a-day eating plan—eat five portions of fruit or vegetables each day. Green leafy vegetables, in particular, are rich in antioxidants. Cabbage, broccoli, Brussels sprouts, cauliflower, and kale contain particularly high levels of antioxidants, which lower the risk of cancer.

Foods that are green in color tend to provide nutrients essential for healthy nerves, muscles, and hormones, while foods red in color protect against cardiovascular disease. Other foods which can also assist in preventing cardiovascular disease and promoting a healthy heart include vitamins E and C, oily fish, garlic, and essential fats, such as extra-virgin olive oil. They help lower blood cholesterol levels and clear arteries. A diet high in fresh fruits and vegetables, and low in salt and saturated fats can considerably reduce heart disease.

Other foods have recognized properties. Certain types of mushrooms are known to boost the immune system. Garlic not only boosts the immune system, but also protects the body against cancer. Live yogurt, too, has healthy properties, as it contains a bacteria that helps the digestive system.

Some foods can help balance the body's hormone levels during menopause. For example, soy regulates hormone levels. Studies have shown that a regular intake of soy can help to protect the body against breast and prostate cancer.

A balanced, healthy diet, rich in fresh fruits and vegetables, carbohydrates, proteins, and essential fats, and low in saturated fat, can help the body protect itself throughout life. It really is worth spending a little extra time and effort when shopping or even just thinking about what to cook.

PANTRY ESSENTIALS
Low-Fat Ingredients for a Healthy Lifestyle

Low-fat cooking has often been associated with the stigma that reducing fat reduces flavor. This is simply not the case, which is great news for those choosing a lower-fat diet. Modern lifestyles are naturally shifting toward healthier diets, so there is no need to compromise on the choice of foods we eat thanks to the increasing number of lower-fat products now available in stores.

The pantry is a good place to start when cooking low-fat meals. Most of us have fairly limited cooking and preparation time available during the week, so choose to experiment on the weekends. When time is of the essence, or friends arrive unannounced, it is always a good idea, especially when following a low-fat diet, to have some key basics in the pantry—foods that are high in flavor and low in fat.

As pantry ingredients keep reasonably well, it really is worth making a trip to a good grocery store. Our society's growing obsession in recent years with travel and food from around the world has led us to seek out new and alternative ingredients with which to experiment and incorporate into our cooking. Consequently, many supermarket chains have had to broaden their product range, and often, these supermarkets carry a wide range of imported ingredients from around the world.

If the local supermarket only carries a limited choice of products, do not despair. The Internet now offers freedom to the food shopaholics among us. There are some fantastic food sites (both local and international) where food can be purchased and delivery arranged online.

When thinking about essentials, think of flavor, something that is going to add to a dish without increasing its fat content. It is worth spending a little bit more money on these products to make flavorful dishes that will help stop the urge to snack on fatty foods.

PANTRY HINTS

There are many different types of pantry ingredients readily available—including myriad varieties of rice and pasta—which can provide much of the carbohydrates required in our daily diets. Store the ingredients in a cool, dark place, and remember to rotate the pantry ingredients. The ingredients will be safe to use for about six months.

BULGUR A cracked wheat that is often used in tabbouleh. Bulgur is an excellent source of complex carbohydrates.

COUSCOUS Now available in instant form, couscous just needs to be covered with boiling water, then fluffed. Couscous is a precooked wheat semolina. Traditional couscous needs to be steamed and is available from health-food stores. This type of couscous contains more nutrients than the instant variety.

DRIED FRUIT The ready-to-eat variety are particularly good, as they are plump, juicy, and do not need to be soaked. They are fantastic puréed into a compote, added to water, heated to make a pie filling, and added to stuffing mixtures. They are also good cooked with meats, rice, or couscous.

FLOURS A useful addition (particularly cornstarch) that can be used to thicken sauces. It is worth mentioning that whole-wheat flour should not be stored for too long at room temperature, as the fats may turn rancid. While not strictly a flour, cornmeal is a very versatile low-fat ingredient, which can be used when making dumplings and gnocchi.

NOODLES Noodles are also very useful and can accompany any Asian dish. They are low in fat and also available in the whole-wheat variety. Rice noodles are available for those who have gluten-free diets and, like pasta noodles, provide slow-release energy to the body.

PASTA It is good to have a mixture of whole-wheat and plain pasta, as well as a wide variety of flavored pastas. Whether fresh (it can also be frozen) or dried, pasta is a versatile ingredient that provides the body with slow-release energy. It comes in many different sizes and shapes; from the tiny tubettini (which can be added to soups to create a much more substantial dish), to penne, rigatoni and conchiglie, up to the larger cannelloni and lasagna sheets.

POT AND PEARL BARLEY Pot barley is the complete barley grain, whereas pearl barley has the outer husk removed. A diet high in cereal grains can help prevent bowel disorders and diseases.

BEANS An important ingredient for the pantry, beans are easy to store, have a very high nutritional value, and are great when added to soups, casseroles, curries, and stews. Beans also act as a thickener, whether flavored or on their own. They come in two forms; either dried (in which case they generally need to be soaked overnight and then cooked before use—it is important to follow the instructions on the package) or canned, which is a convenient time-saver because the preparation of dried beans can take a long time. If buying canned beans, try to buy the variety in water with no added salt or sugar. These simply need to be drained and rinsed before being added to a dish.

Kidney beans, cranberry beans, lima beans, fava beans, split peas, and lentils all make tasty additions to any dish. Baked beans are a favorite with everyone, and many stores now stock the organic variety, which have no added salt or sugar but are instead sweetened with fruit juice.

When boiling previously dried beans, remember that salt should not be added, as this will make the skins tough and inedible. Lentils are a smaller variety. They often have mottled skins and are particularly good for cooking in slow dishes, as they hold their shape and firm texture particularly well.

RICE Basmati and Thai fragrant rice are well suited to Thai and Indian curries, as the fine grains absorb the sauce and their delicate creaminess balances the pungency of the spices. There is also risotto rice, and many types are available,

depending on whether the risotto is meant to accompany meat, fish, or vegetable dishes. When cooked, rice swells to create a substantial low-fat dish. Instant rice, both plain and brown, is great for casseroles and for stuffing meat, fish, and vegetables, as it holds its shape and firmness. Pudding rice can be used in a variety of ways to create an irresistible dessert.

STOCK Good-quality stock is a must in low-fat cooking, as it provides a good flavor base for many dishes. Many stores now carry a variety of fresh and organic stocks which, although they need refrigeration, are probably one of the most time- and effort-saving ingredients available.

There is also a fairly large range of dried stock, perhaps the best being bouillon, a high-quality form of stock (available in powder or liquid form) that can be added to any dish, whether it be a sauce, casserole, pie, or soup.

Many people enjoy meals that can be prepared and cooked in 30–45 minutes, so helpful ingredients that kick-start a sauce are great. A good quality puréed tomato sauce or canned plum tomatoes can act as the foundation for any sauce, as can a good-quality green or red pesto. Other handy pantry additions include tapenade, mustard, and anchovies. These ingredients have very distinctive tastes and are particularly flavorful. Roasted red bell pepper sauce and sun-dried tomato paste, which tends to be sweeter and more intensely flavored than the regular tomato paste, are also extremely useful.

VINEGAR Another worthwhile pantry essential, and with so many uses, it is worth purchasing a really good-quality balsamic and wine vinegar. Herbs and spices are a must, so it is worth taking a look at the section on pages 14–15. Using herbs when cooking at home should reduce the temptation to buy premade sauces. Often, these types of sauces contain large amounts of sugar and additives.

Yeast extract is also a good pantry ingredient, as it can pep up sauces, soups, and casseroles, and add a little substance—particularly to vegetarian dishes.

Eastern flavors offer a lot of scope where low-fat cooking is concerned. Flavorings such as fish sauce, soy sauce, red and green curry paste, and Chinese rice wine will enhance any dish.

For those who are incredibly short on time or who rarely shop, it is now possible to purchase prepared, crushed garlic, ginger, and chili (now available in jars that can be kept in the refrigerator).

As well as these pantry additions, many stores and supermarkets provide a wide choice of products and carry a wide range of low-fat items. Where possible, invest in the leanest cut of meat, and substitute saturated fats, such as cream, butter, and cheese, with low-fat or reduced-fat alternatives, such as light sour cream, butter, and cheese.

HERBS AND SPICES

In a culture where fast food, premade meals, and processed foods are popular, people sometimes feel daunted by the prospect of a low-fat diet. It is a common myth that the low-fat diet is less appealing or appetizing. This is partly due, however, to the fact that the palate becomes used to rich sauces and processed food with additives and artificial flavorings.

Someone accustomed to a high proportion of fried food may find it difficult to adjust to a diet that maximizes nutrition through steaming, boiling, baking, or broiling. The use of herbs and spices is good news for the low-fat diet and can make all the difference between a bland and a tasty dish, helping the individual to stick to a low-fat diet.

Herbs are easy to grow and a garden is not needed, as they can easily thrive on a small patio, window box, or even on a windowsill. It is worth the effort to plant a few herbs, as they do not require much attention or nurturing. The reward will be a range of fresh herbs available whenever needed and fresh flavors to add to any dish that is being prepared.

While fresh herbs should be picked or bought as close as possible to the time of use, dried herbs and spices will usually keep for around six months.

The best idea is to buy little and often, and to store the herbs in airtight jars in a cool, dark cupboard. Fresh herbs tend to have a milder flavor than dried, and equate to around one level tablespoon of fresh to one level teaspoon of dried. As a result, quantities used in cooking should be adjusted accordingly. A variety of herbs and spices, and their uses are listed below.

ALLSPICE

The dark allspice berries come whole or ground, and have a flavor similar to that of cinnamon, cloves, and nutmeg. Although not the same as mixed spices, allspice can be used with pickles, relishes, cakes, and milk desserts, or whole in meat and fish dishes.

ANISEED

Aniseed comes in whole seeds or ground. It has a strong aroma and flavor, and should be used sparingly in baking and salad dressings.

BASIL

Best fresh, but also available in dried form, basil can be used raw or cooked and works well in many dishes, but is particularly well suited to tomato-based dishes and sauces, salads, and Mediterranean dishes.

BAY LEAVES

Bay leaves are available in fresh or dried form, as well as ground. They make up part of a bouquet garni and are particularly delicious when added to meat and poultry dishes, soups, casseroles, vegetable dishes, and stuffing. They also impart a spicy flavor to milk desserts and egg custards.

BOUQUET GARNI

Bouquet garni is a bouquet of fresh herbs tied with a piece of string or in a small piece of cheesecloth. It is used to flavor casseroles, stews, and stocks or sauces. The herbs that are normally used are parsley, thyme, and bay leaves.

CARAWAY SEEDS

Caraway seeds have a warm, sweet taste, and are often used in breads and cakes, but are delicious with cabbage dishes and pickles, as well.

CAYENNE

Cayenne is the powdered form of a red chili pepper said to be native to Cayenne. It is similar in appearance to paprika and can be used sparingly to add a fiery kick to many dishes.

CARDAMOM

Cardamom has a distinctive sweet, rich taste, and can be bought whole in the pod, in seed form, or ground. This aromatic spice is delicious in curries, rice, cakes, and cookies, and is great served with rice pudding and fruit.

CHERVIL

Reminiscent of parsley and available either in fresh or dried form, chervil has a faintly sweet, spicy flavor, and is particularly good in soups, cheese dishes, stews, and with eggs.

CHILI

Available whole, fresh, dried, and in powdered form, red chilies tend to be sweeter in taste than their green counterparts. They are particularly associated with Spanish and Mexican-style cooking and curries, but are also delicious with pickles, dips, sauces, and in pizza toppings.

CHIVES

Best used when fresh, but also available in dried form, this member of the onion family is ideal for use when a delicate onion flavor is required. Chives are good with eggs, cheese, fish, and vegetable dishes. They also work well as a garnish for soups, meat, and vegetable dishes.

CINNAMON

Cinnamon comes in the form of reddish-brown sticks of bark from an evergreen tree and has a sweet, pungent aroma. Either whole or ground, cinnamon is delicious in cakes and milk desserts, particularly with apples, and is used in mulled wine and for preserving.

CLOVES

Mainly used whole, although available ground, cloves have a very warm, sweet, pungent aroma, and can be used to stud roast ham and pork, in mulled wine and punch, and when pickling fruit. When ground, they can be used in making mincemeat and cookies.

CORIANDER/CILANTRO

Coriander seeds have an orangey flavor and are available whole or ground. Coriander is particularly delicious (whether whole or coarsely ground) in casseroles, curries, and as a pickling spice. The fresh leaves (called cilantro) are used to flavor spicy, aromatic dishes, as well as a garnish.

CUMIN

Also available ground or as whole seeds, cumin has a strong, slightly bitter flavor. It is one of the main ingredients in curry powder and complements many fish, meat, and rice dishes.

DILL

Dill leaves are available fresh or dried and have a mild flavor, while the seeds are slightly bitter. Dill is good with salmon, new potatoes, and in sauces. The seeds are good in pickles and vegetable dishes.

FENNEL

Whole seeds or ground, fennel has a fragrant, sweet, aniseed flavor, and is sometimes known as the "fish herb" because it complements fish dishes well.

GINGER

Ginger comes in many forms, but primarily as a fresh root and in dried ground form, which can be used in baking, curries, pickles, sauces, and Chinese cooking.

LEMONGRASS

Available fresh and dried, with a subtle, aromatic, lemony flavor, lemongrass is essential to Thai cooking. It is also delicious when added to soups, poultry, and fish dishes.

MACE

The outer husk of nutmeg has a milder nutmeg flavor and can be used in pickles, cheese dishes, stewed fruits, sauces, and hot punch.

MARJORAM

Often dried, marjoram has a sweet, slightly spicy flavor, which tastes fantastic when added to stuffing, meat, or tomato-based dishes.

MINT

Available fresh or dried, it has a strong, sweet aroma, which is delicious in a sauce or jelly served with lamb. It is also great with fresh peas, as well as with new potatoes.

MUSTARD SEED

These yellow and brown seeds are available whole or ground and are often found in pickles, relishes, cheese dishes, dressings, curries, and as an accompaniment to meat.

NUTMEG

The large whole seeds have a warm, sweet taste and complement custards, milk desserts, cheese dishes, parsnips, and creamy soups.

OREGANO

The strongly flavored dried leaves are similar to marjoram and are used extensively in Italian and Greek cooking.

PAPRIKA

Paprika often comes in two varieties. One is quite sweet and mild, and the other has a slight bite to it. Paprika is made from the fruit of the bell pepper and is good in meat and poultry dishes, as well as a garnish. The rule of buying herbs and spices little and often applies particularly to paprika, as it does not keep particularly well.

PARSLEY

The stems, as well as the leaves, of parsley can be used to complement most savory dishes, as they contain the most flavor. They can also be used as a garnish.

PEPPER

This comes in white and black peppercorns and is best freshly ground. Both add flavor to most dishes, sauces, and gravies. Black pepper has a more robust flavor, while white pepper has a much more delicate flavor.

POPPY SEEDS

These little, grey-black colored seeds impart a sweet, nutty flavor when added to cookies, vegetable dishes, dressings, and cheese dishes.

ROSEMARY

Delicious fresh or dried, the small needle-like leaves have a sweet aroma, which is particularly good with lamb, stuffing, and vegetable dishes. Also delicious when added to charcoal on the barbecue to give a piquant flavour to meat and corn-on-the-cob.

SAFFRON

Deep orange in color, saffron is traditionally used in paella, rice, and cakes, but is also delicious with poultry. Saffron is the most expensive of all spices.

SAGE

The fresh or dried leaves have a pungent, slightly bitter taste, which is delicious with pork and poultry, sausages, stuffing, and with stuffed pasta when tossed in a little butter and fresh sage.

SAVORY

This herb resembles thyme, but has a softer flavor that particularly complements all types of fish and beans.

SESAME

Sesame seeds have a nutty taste, especially when toasted, and are delicious in baking, on salads, or with Asian cooking.

TARRAGON

The fresh or dried leaves of tarragon have a sweet, aromatic taste, which is particularly good with poultry, shellfish, fish, creamy sauces, and stuffing.

THYME

Available fresh or dried, thyme has a pungent flavor and is included in bouquet garni. It complements many meat and poultry dishes, as well as stuffing.

TURMERIC

Turmeric is obtained from the root of a lily from southeast Asia. This root is ground and has a brilliant yellow color. It has a bitter, peppery flavor, and is often combined for use in curry powder and mustard. Also delicious in pickles, relishes, and dressings.

MUSHROOM & SHERRY SOUP

INGREDIENTS

Serves 4

4 slices day-old white bread
1 tsp. lemon zest
1 tbsp. lemon juice
salt and freshly ground
 black pepper
1¾ cups assorted wild
 mushrooms, lightly rinsed
1¾ cups baby button
 mushrooms, wiped

2 tsp. olive oil
1 garlic clove, peeled
 and crushed
6 scallions, trimmed
 and diagonally sliced
2½ cups chicken stock
4 tbsp. dry sherry
1 tbsp. freshly cut chives, to
 garnish

1 Preheat the oven to 350° F. Remove the crusts from the bread and cut the bread into small cubes.

2 In a large bowl, toss the cubes of bread with the lemon zest and juice, 2 tablespoons of water, and plenty of freshly ground black pepper.

3 Spread the bread cubes onto a lightly greased baking sheet and cook in the preheated oven for 20 minutes until golden and crisp.

4 If the wild mushrooms are small, leave some whole. Otherwise, thinly slice all the mushrooms and set aside.

5 Heat the oil in a saucepan. Add the garlic and scallions, and cook for 1–2 minutes.

6 Add the mushrooms and cook for 3–4 minutes until they start to soften. Add the chicken stock and stir to mix.

7 Bring to a boil, then reduce the heat to a gentle simmer. Cover the pan with a lid and cook for 10 minutes.

8 Stir in the sherry, and season to taste with a little salt and pepper. Pour into warmed bowls, sprinkle the chives on top, and serve the soup immediately with the lemon croutons.

HELPFUL HINT

To achieve very fine shreds, use a zester, available from all kitchen stores. Or, thinly peel the fruit with a vegetable peeler, then shred with a small, sharp knife. When grating fruit, use a clean, dry pastry brush to remove the rind from the grater.

CHINESE CHICKEN SOUP

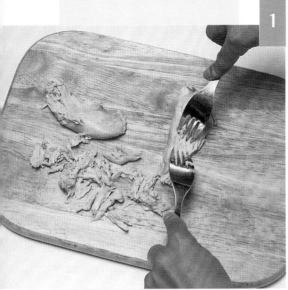

INGREDIENTS
Serves 4

8 oz. cooked chicken
1 tsp. oil
6 scallions, trimmed
 and diagonally sliced
1 red chili, seeded and
 finely chopped
1 garlic clove, peeled
 and crushed
1-in. piece fresh ginger, peeled
 and finely grated
4 cups chicken stock

1½ cups medium
 egg noodles
1 carrot, peeled and cut
 into matchsticks
¾ cup bean sprouts
2 tbsp. soy sauce
1 tbsp. fish sauce
fresh cilantro leaves,
 to garnish

1 Remove any skin from the chicken. Place on a chopping board and use 2 forks to tear the chicken into fine shreds.

2 Heat the oil in a large saucepan and fry the scallions and chili for 1 minute.

3 Add the garlic and ginger, and cook for another minute.

4 Stir in the chicken stock and gradually bring the mixture to a boil.

5 Break up the noodles a little and add to the boiling stock, along with the carrot.

6 Stir to mix, then reduce the heat to a simmer and cook for 3–4 minutes.

7 Add the shredded chicken, bean sprouts, soy sauce, and fish sauce, and stir.

8 Cook for an additional 2–3 minutes until piping hot. Spoon the soup into bowls and sprinkle with a few fresh cilantro leaves. Serve immediately.

TASTY TIP

If possible, buy corn-fed chicken for this recipe. Since this soup is chicken stock-based, the use of corn-fed chicken will make the soup much more flavorful.
For added nutritional value, substitute the egg noodles with the whole-wheat variety and use sesame oil in step 2. Increase the vegetable content by adding ¾ cups each of water chestnuts and bamboo shoots, and ½ cup of snow peas and baby corn in step 7.

CARROT & GINGER SOUP

INGREDIENTS   Serves 4

4 slices of bread,
  crusts removed
1 tsp. yeast extract
2 tsp. olive oil
1 onion, peeled and chopped
1 garlic clove, peeled
  and crushed
½ tsp. ground ginger
2½ cups carrots, peeled
  and chopped
4 cups vegetable stock

1-in. piece of ginger, peeled
  and finely grated
salt and freshly ground
  black pepper
1 tbsp. lemon juice

TO GARNISH:
chives
lemon zest

1 Preheat the oven to 350° F. Coarsely chop the bread. Dissolve the yeast extract in 2 tablespoons of warm water, and mix with the bread.

2 Spread the bread cubes over a lightly greased baking sheet and cook for 20 minutes, turning halfway through. Remove from the oven and set aside.

3 Heat the oil in a large saucepan. Gently cook the onion and garlic for 3–4 minutes.

4 Stir in the ground ginger and cook for 1 minute to release the flavor.

5 Add the chopped carrots, then stir in the stock and the fresh ginger. Simmer gently for 15 minutes.

6 Remove from the heat and allow to cool slightly. Blend until smooth, then season to taste with salt and pepper. Stir in the lemon juice. Garnish with the chives and lemon zest, and serve immediately.

TASTY TIP

This soup would be delicious for special occasions if served with a spoonful of lightly whipped cream or low-fat sour cream. Serve with slices of bruschetta, which can be easily made by lightly broiling thick slices of ciabatta bread on both sides. While still warm, rub the top of the bruschetta with a whole, peeled clove of garlic, and drizzle with a little good-quality extra-virgin olive oil.

ITALIAN BEAN SOUP

2

INGREDIENTS   Serves 4

2 tsp. olive oil
1 leek, washed and chopped
1 garlic clove, peeled
   and crushed
2 tsp. dried oregano
¾ cup green beans, trimmed
   and cut into bite-size pieces

14-oz. can lima beans, drained
   and rinsed
¾ cup small pasta shapes
4 cups vegetable stock
8 cherry tomatoes
salt and freshly ground
   black pepper
3 tbsp. freshly torn basil

5

1 Heat the oil in a large saucepan. Add the leek, garlic, and oregano, and cook for 5 minutes, stirring occasionally.

2 Stir in the green beans and the lima beans. Sprinkle in the pasta and pour in the stock.

3 Bring the stock mixture to a boil, then reduce the heat to a simmer.

4 Cook for 12–15 minutes or until the vegetables are tender and the pasta is cooked to al dente. Stir occasionally.

6

5 In a heavy skillet, fry the tomatoes over a high heat until they soften and the skins begin to blacken.

6 Gently crush the tomatoes in the skillet with the back of a spoon, and add to the soup.

7 Season to taste with salt and pepper. Stir in the shredded basil and serve immediately.

TASTY TIP

This soup will taste even better the day after it has been made. Make the soup the day before you intend to serve it, and add a little extra stock when reheating.

FOOD FACT

The majority of Italian cooking takes advantage of the abundance of freshly grown herbs, especially when used in tomato-based dishes. With a few exceptions, it is worth trying to use fresh herbs to draw out the other flavors of the dish. However, if you decide to use dried herbs, remember that they are much more pungent. 1 teaspoon of dried herbs equals roughly 1 tablespoon of fresh herbs.

TOMATO & BASIL SOUP

INGREDIENTS   Serves 4

7 medium, ripe tomatoes,
  cut in half
2 garlic cloves
1 tsp. olive oil
1 tbsp. balsamic vinegar
1 tbsp. dark brown sugar
1 tbsp. tomato paste

1¼ cups vegetable stock
6 tbsp. low-fat plain yogurt
2 tbsp. freshly chopped basil
salt and freshly ground
  black pepper
small basil leaves,
  to garnish

1 Preheat the oven to 400° F. Evenly spread the tomato halves and unpeeled garlic in a single layer in a large roasting pan.

2 Mix the oil and vinegar together. Drizzle over the tomatoes and sprinkle with the dark brown sugar.

3 Roast the tomatoes in the preheated oven for 20 minutes until tender and lightly charred in places.

4 Remove from the oven and allow to cool slightly. When cool enough to handle, squeeze the softened flesh of the garlic from the papery skin. Place with the charred tomatoes in a strainer over a saucepan.

5 Press the garlic and tomato through the strainer with the back of a wooden spoon.

6 When all the flesh has been strained, add the tomato paste and the vegetable stock to the pan. Heat gently, stirring occasionally.

7 In a small bowl beat the yogurt and basil together, and season to taste with salt and pepper. Stir the basil yogurt into the soup. Garnish with basil leaves and serve immediately.

TASTY TIP

Use the sweetest type of tomatoes available, as it makes a big difference to the flavor of the soup. Many supermarkets now stock special tomatoes, grown slowly and matured for longer on the vine to give them an intense flavor. If these are unavailable, add a little extra sugar to bring out the flavor.

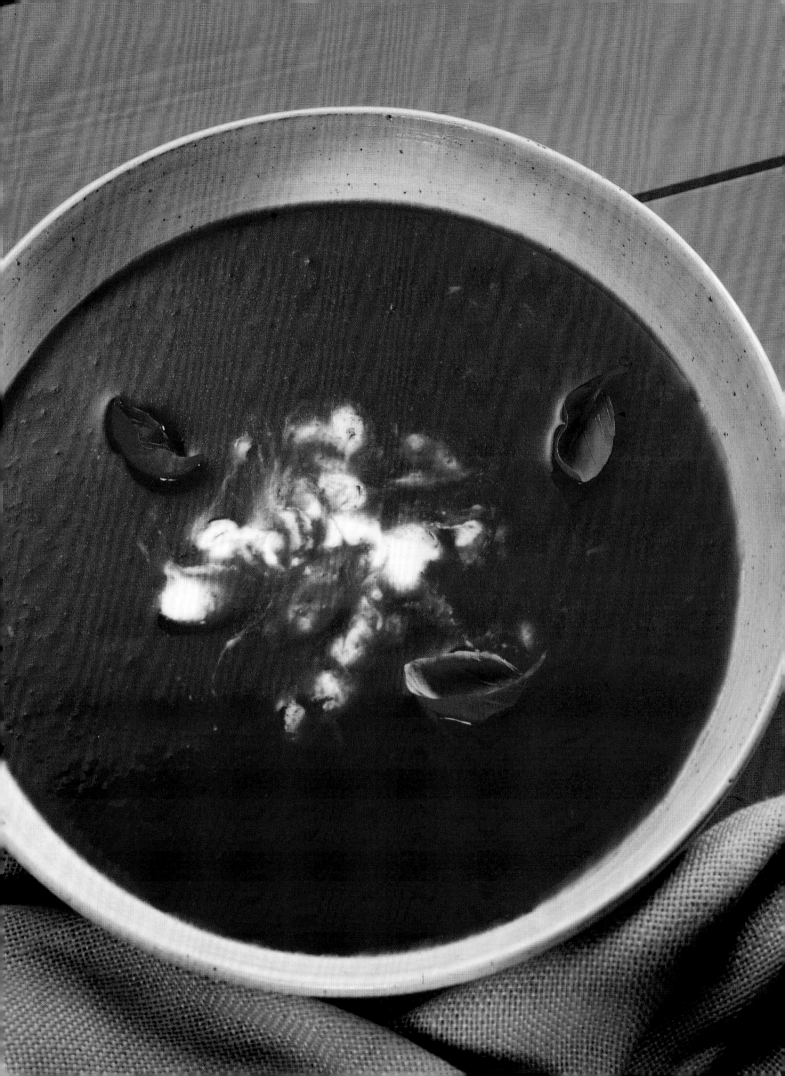

SHRIMP & CHILI SOUP

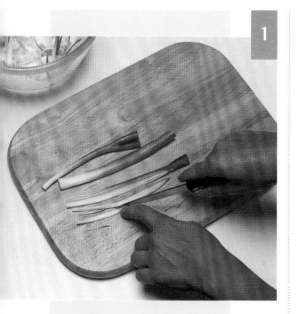

INGREDIENTS   Serves 4

2 scallions, trimmed
8 oz. whole, raw jumbo
   shrimp
3 cups fish stock
2 tsp. finely grated lime rind
1 tbsp. lime juice
1 tbsp. fish sauce

1 red chili, seeded
   and chopped
1 tbsp. soy sauce
1 lemongrass stalk
2 tbsp. rice vinegar
4 tbsp. freshly chopped
   cilantro

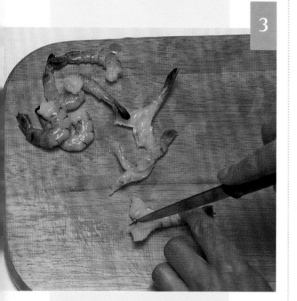

1 To make the scallion curls, finely shred the scallions lengthwise. Place in a bowl of ice-cold water and set aside.

2 Remove the heads and shells from the shrimp, leaving the tails intact.

3 Split the shrimp almost in two to form a butterfly shape, and individually remove the black vein that runs down the back of each.

4 In a large saucepan, heat the stock with the lime rind and juice, fish sauce, chili, and soy sauce.

5 Bruise the lemongrass by crushing it along its length with a rolling pin, then add to the stock mixture.

6 When the stock mixture is boiling, add the shrimp and cook until they are pink.

7 Remove the lemongrass and add the rice vinegar and cilantro.

8 Spoon into bowls and garnish with the scallion curls. Serve immediately.

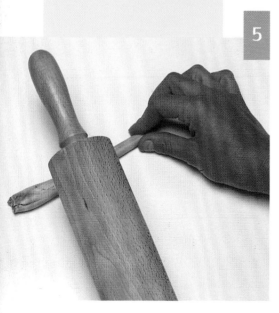

TASTY TIP

For a more substantial dish, cook ¼ cup Thai fragrant rice for 12–15 minutes or until just cooked. Drain, then place a little in the soup bowl and spoon the prepared soup on top.

CURRIED PARSNIP SOUP

INGREDIENTS   Serves 4

1 tsp. cumin seeds
2 tsp. coriander seeds
1 tsp. oil
1 onion, peeled and chopped
1 garlic clove, peeled
   and crushed
½ tsp. turmeric
¼ tsp. chili powder
1 cinnamon stick

2 cups parsnips, peeled and
   chopped
4 cups vegetable stock
salt and freshly ground
   black pepper
2–3 tbsp. low-fat plain yogurt,
   to serve
fresh cilantro leaves,
   to garnish

1 In a small skillet, fry the cumin and coriander seeds over a moderately high heat for 1–2 minutes. Shake the skillet during cooking until the seeds are lightly toasted.

2 Set aside until cooled. Grind the toasted seeds with a mortar and pestle.

3 Heat the oil in a saucepan. Cook the onion until softened and starting to turn golden.

4 Add the garlic, turmeric, chili powder, and cinnamon stick to the pan. Continue to cook for an additional minute.

5 Add the parsnips and stir well. Pour in the stock and bring to a boil. Cover and simmer for 15 minutes or until the parsnips are cooked.

6 Allow the soup to cool. Once cooled, remove the cinnamon stick and discard.

7 Blend the soup in a food processor until very smooth.

8 Transfer to a saucepan and reheat gently. Season to taste with salt and pepper. Garnish with fresh cilantro leaves, and serve immediately with yogurt.

FOOD FACT

Parsnips vary in color from pale yellow to a creamy white. They are at their best when they are the size of a large carrot. If larger, remove the central core, which can be woody.

MUSHROOM & RED WINE PÂTÉ

INGREDIENTS   Serves 4

3 large slices of white bread,
  crusts removed
2 tsp. oil
1 small onion, peeled and
  finely chopped
1 garlic clove, peeled
  and crushed
3¾ cup button mushrooms,
  wiped and finely chopped
⅔ cup red wine
½ tsp. dried mixed herbs

1 tbsp. freshly chopped
  parsley
salt and freshly ground
  black pepper
2 tbsp. low-fat cream cheese

TO SERVE:
finely chopped cucumber
finely chopped tomato

1 Preheat the oven to 350° F.
Cut the bread in half
diagonally. Place the bread
triangles on a baking sheet and
cook for 10 minutes.

2 Remove from the oven and
split each bread triangle in
half to make 12 triangles, and
return to the oven until golden
and crisp. Allow to cool on a wire
rack.

3 Heat the oil in a saucepan
and gently cook the onion
and garlic until transparent.

4 Add the mushrooms and
cook, stirring for 3–4
minutes or until the mushroom
juices start to run.

5 Stir the wine and herbs into
the mushroom mixture and
bring to a boil. Reduce the heat
and simmer uncovered until all
the liquid is absorbed.

6 Remove from the heat and
season to taste with salt and
pepper. Allow to cool.

7 When cold, beat in the cream
cheese and season lightly.
Place in a small, clean bowl and
chill in the refrigerator until
needed. Serve the toast triangles
with the cucumber and tomato.

TASTY TIP

This pâté is also delicious
served as a bruschetta
topping. Toast slices of
ciabatta, generously spread
the pâté on top, and garnish
with a little arugula.

THAI FISH CAKES

INGREDIENTS   Serves 4

1 red chili, seeded
  and coarsely chopped
4 tbsp. coarsely chopped
  fresh cilantro
1 garlic clove, peeled
  and crushed
2 scallions, trimmed
  and coarsely chopped
1 lemongrass, outer
  leaves discarded and
  coarsely chopped

3 oz. shrimp, defrosted if
  frozen
10 oz. cod fillet, skinned, pin
  bones removed, and cubed
salt and freshly ground
  black pepper
sweet chili dipping sauce,
  to serve

1 Preheat the oven to 375° F. Place the chili, cilantro, garlic, scallions, and lemongrass in a food processor, and blend together.

2 Pat the shrimp and cod dry with paper towels.

3 Add to the food processor and blend until the mixture is coarsely chopped.

4 Season to taste with salt and pepper, and blend to mix.

5 Dampen your hands, then shape heaping tablespoons of the mixture into 12 little patties.

6 Place the patties on a lightly greased baking sheet, and cook in the preheated oven for 12–15 minutes or until piping hot and cooked through. Turn the patties over halfway through the cooking time.

7 Serve the fish cakes immediately with the sweet chili sauce for dipping.

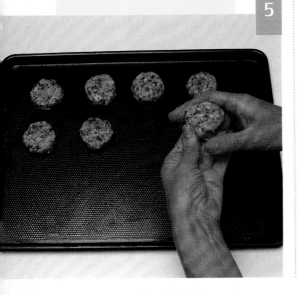

TASTY TIP

A horseradish dip could be used in place of the sweet chili sauce, if a creamier dip is preferred. Mix together 2 tablespoons of grated horseradish (from a jar) with 3 tablespoons each of plain yogurt and low-calorie mayonnaise. Add 3 finely chopped scallions, a squeeze of lime, and salt and pepper to taste.

HOISIN CHICKEN PANCAKES

INGREDIENTS   Serves 4

3 tbsp. hoisin sauce
1 garlic clove, peeled
    and crushed
1-in. piece ginger, peeled and
    finely grated
1 tbsp. soy sauce
1 tsp. sesame oil
salt and freshly ground
    black pepper

4 skinless chicken thighs
½ cucumber, peeled (optional)
12 store-bought Chinese
    pancakes
6 scallions, trimmed
    and cut lengthwise
sweet chili dipping sauce,
    to serve

1 Preheat the oven to 375°F. In a nonmetallic bowl, mix the hoisin sauce with the garlic, ginger, soy sauce, sesame oil, and seasoning.

2 Add the chicken thighs and coat in the mixture. Cover loosely with plastic wrap, and leave in the refrigerator to marinate for 3–4 hours, turning the chicken occasionally.

3 Remove the chicken from the marinade and place in a roasting pan. Set the marinade aside. Cook in the preheated oven for 30 minutes, basting occasionally with the marinade.

4 Cut the cucumber in half lengthwise, and remove the seeds by running a teaspoon down the center to scoop them out. Cut into thin pieces.

5 Place the pancakes in a steamer to warm, according to package instructions. Thinly slice the hot chicken, and arrange on a plate with the shredded scallions, cucumber, and pancakes.

6 Place a spoonful of the chicken in the center of each warmed pancake, and top with pieces of cucumber, scallion, and some of the dipping sauce. Roll up and serve immediately.

TASTY TIP

For those with wheat allergies or who want to make this tasty dish more substantial, stir-fry the scallions and cucumber pieces in a little peanut oil. Add a carrot cut into batons and mix in the thinly sliced chicken and extra marinade (as prepared in step 3). Serve with steamed rice—Thai fragrant rice is particularly good.

ROASTED RED BELL PEPPER, TOMATO, & RED ONION SOUP

INGREDIENTS   Serves 4

fine spray of oil
2 large red bell peppers,
    seeded and coarsely
    chopped
1 red onion, peeled and
    coarsely chopped
2 medium tomatoes, halved

1 small, crusty French loaf
1 garlic clove, peeled
2½ cups vegetable stock
salt and freshly ground
    black pepper
1 tsp. Worcestershire sauce
4 tbsp. low-fat sour cream

1 Preheat the oven to 375° F. Spray a large roasting pan with the oil, and place the bell peppers and the onion in the base. Cook in the preheated oven for 10 minutes. Add the tomatoes, and cook for an additional 20 minutes or until the bell peppers are soft.

2 Cut the bread into ½ inch slices. Cut the garlic clove in half and rub the cut edge of the garlic over the bread.

3 Place all the bread slices on a large baking sheet, and cook in the oven for 10 minutes, turning halfway through, until golden and crisp.

4 Remove the vegetables from the oven and allow to cool slightly, then blend in a food processor until smooth. Strain the vegetable mixture through a large strainer into a saucepan to remove the seeds and skin. Add the stock, season to taste with salt and pepper, and stir to mix. Heat the soup gently until piping hot.

5 In a small bowl, beat together the Worcestershire sauce with the sour cream.

6 Pour the soup into warmed bowls and swirl a spoonful of the sour cream mixture into each bowl. Serve immediately with the garlic toast.

HELPFUL HINT

A quick way to remove the skin from bell peppers once they have been roasted or broiled is to place them in a plastic bag. Leave for 10 minutes or until cool enough to handle, then peel the skin away from the flesh.

HOT HERBED MUSHROOMS

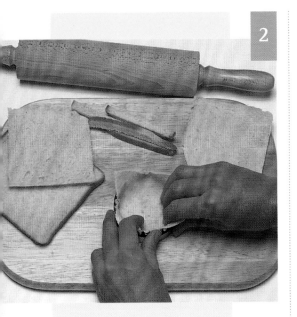

INGREDIENTS — Serves 4

4 thin slices of white bread, crusts removed
1¾ cups chestnut mushrooms, wiped and sliced
1¾ cups oyster mushrooms, wiped
1 garlic clove, peeled and crushed
1 tsp. mustard

1¼ cups chicken stock
salt and freshly ground black pepper
1 tbsp. freshly chopped parsley
1 tbsp. freshly cut chives, plus extra to garnish
mixed lettuce leaves, to serve

1 Preheat the oven to 350° F. With a rolling pin, roll each piece of bread out as thinly as possible.

2 Press each piece of bread into a 4-inch tartlet pan. Push each piece firmly down, then bake in the preheated oven for 20 minutes.

3 Place the mushrooms in a skillet with the garlic, mustard, and chicken stock, and stir-fry over a moderate heat until the mushrooms are tender and the liquid is reduced by half.

4 Using a slotted spoon, carefully remove the mushrooms from the skillet, and transfer to a heat-resistant dish. Cover with foil and place in the bottom of the oven to keep the mushrooms warm.

5 Boil the remaining juices until reduced to a thick sauce. Season with salt and pepper.

6 Stir the parsley and chives into the mushroom mixture.

7 Place one bread tartlet shell on each plate, and divide the mushroom mixture among them.

8 Spoon over the juices, garnish with the chives, and serve immediately with mixed lettuce leaves.

FOOD FACT

Mushrooms are an extremely nutritious food, rich in vitamins and minerals, which help to boost our immune system.
This recipe could be adapted to include shiitake mushrooms, which studies have shown can significantly boost and protect the body's immune system, and can also strengthen the body's protection against cancer.

CILANTRO CHICKEN & SOY SAUCE CAKES

INGREDIENTS   Serves 4

¼ cucumber, peeled
1 shallot, peeled and
  thinly sliced
6 radishes, trimmed and sliced
12 oz. skinless, boneless
  chicken thigh
4 tbsp. coarsely chopped
  fresh cilantro
2 scallions, trimmed and
  coarsely chopped

1 red chili, seeded
  and chopped
2 tsp. finely grated lime rind
2 tbsp. soy sauce
1 tbsp. sugar
2 tbsp. rice vinegar
1 red chili, seeded and finely
  sliced
freshly chopped cilantro,
  to garnish

1 Preheat the oven to 375° F. Halve the peeled cucumber lengthwise, remove the seeds, and dice.

2 In a bowl, mix the shallot and radishes together. Chill until ready to serve.

3 Place the chicken thighs in a food processor, and blend until coarsely chopped.

4 Add the cilantro and scallions to the chicken with the chili, lime zest, and soy sauce. Blend again until mixed.

5 Using slightly damp hands, shape the chicken mixture into 12 small rounds.

6 Place the rounds on a lightly greased baking sheet and cook in the preheated oven for 15 minutes or until golden.

7 In a small saucepan, heat the sugar with 2 tablespoons of water until dissolved. Simmer until syrupy.

8 Remove from the heat and allow to cool a little, then stir in the vinegar and chili slices. Pour over the cucumber, radish, and shallot salad. Garnish with the freshly chopped cilantro, and serve the chicken cakes with the salad immediately.

FOOD FACT

In this recipe, the chicken cakes can be altered so that half chicken and half lean pork is used. This alters the flavor of the dish and works really well if a small 1-inch piece of fresh ginger is grated and added in Step 4.

ROASTED EGGPLANT DIP WITH PITA STRIPS

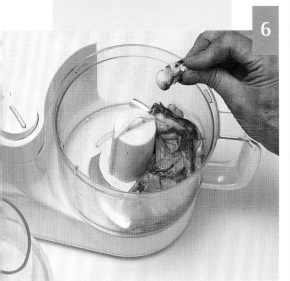

INGREDIENTS — Serves 4

4 pita breads
2 large eggplants
1 garlic clove, peeled
¼ tsp. sesame oil
1 tbsp. lemon juice

½ tsp. cumin
salt and freshly ground
  black pepper
2 tbsp. freshly chopped parsley
fresh lettuce leaves, to serve

1 Preheat the oven to 350° F. On a chopping board, cut the pita breads into strips, and spread in a single layer onto a large baking sheet.

2 Cook in the preheated oven for 15 minutes or until golden brown and crisp. Allow to cool on a wire rack.

3 Trim the eggplants, rinse lightly, and set aside. Heat a griddle pan until almost smoking. Cook the eggplants and garlic for about 15 minutes.

4 Turn the eggplants frequently until very tender, with wrinkled and charred skins. Remove from the heat. Let cool.

5 When the eggplants are cool enough to handle, cut in half, and scoop out the cooked flesh and place in a food processor.

6 Squeeze the softened garlic flesh from the papery skin, and add to the eggplant in the food processor.

7 Blend the eggplant and garlic until smooth, then add the sesame oil, lemon juice, and cumin, and blend again to mix.

8 Season to taste with salt and pepper, stir in the parsley, and serve with the pita strips and mixed lettuce leaves.

FOOD FACT

This dish is a variation on the traditional Arabic dish known as *baba ghanouj*, which translates to "spoiled old man." As well as being great with pita strips or grissini, this dish is fantastic as a side dish when served hot.

GRILLED GARLIC & LEMON SQUID

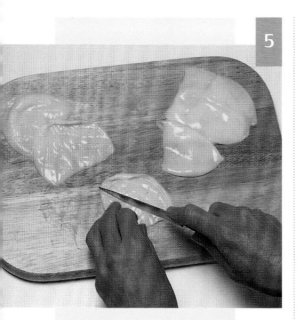

INGREDIENTS   Serves 4

½ cup long-grain rice
1¼ cups fish stock
8 oz. squid, cleaned
1 tbsp. grated lemon rind
1 garlic clove, peeled
  and crushed
1 shallot, peeled and
  finely chopped

2 tbsp. freshly chopped
  cilantro
2 tbsp. lemon juice
salt and freshly ground
  black pepper

1 Rinse the rice until the water runs clear, then place in a saucepan with the stock.

2 Bring to a boil, then reduce the heat. Cover and simmer gently for 10 minutes.

3 Turn off the heat and leave the saucepan covered so the rice can steam while you cook the squid.

4 Remove the tentacles from the squid, and set aside.

5 Cut the body cavity in half. Using the tip of a small, sharp knife, score the inside flesh of the body cavity in a diamond pattern. Do not cut all the way through.

6 Mix the lemon rind, crushed garlic, and chopped shallot together.

7 Place the squid in a shallow bowl, sprinkle the lemon mixture on top, and stir.

8 Heat a griddle pan until almost smoking. Cook the squid for 3–4 minutes until cooked through, then slice.

9 Sprinkle with the cilantro and lemon juice. Season to taste with salt and pepper. Drain the rice and serve immediately with the squid.

HELPFUL HINT

To prepare squid, peel the tentacles from the squid's pouch, and cut away the head just below the eye. Discard the head. Remove the quill and the soft innards from the squid, and discard. Peel off any dark skin that covers the squid, and discard. Rinse the tentacles and pouch thoroughly. The squid is now ready to use.

CREAMY SALMON WITH DILL IN PHYLLO BASKETS

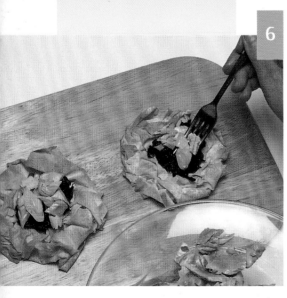

INGREDIENTS   Serves 4

1 bay leaf
6 black peppercorns
1 large sprig of fresh parsley
6 oz. salmon fillet
4 large sheets phyllo pastry
fine spray of oil

2½ cups baby spinach leaves
8 tbsp. low-fat sour cream
2 tsp. mustard
2 tbsp. freshly chopped dill
salt and freshly ground
black pepper

1 Preheat the oven to 400° F. Place the bay leaf, peppercorns, parsley, and salmon in a large skillet, and add enough water to barely cover the fish.

2 Bring to a boil, reduce the heat, and cook the fish for 5 minutes until it flakes easily. Remove from the skillet. Set aside.

3 Spray each sheet of phyllo pastry lightly with the oil. Scrunch up the pastry to make a nest shape approximately 5 inches in diameter.

4 Place on a lightly greased baking sheet, and cook in the preheated oven for 10 minutes until golden and crisp.

5 Blanch the baby spinach leaves in a saucepan of lightly salted boiling water for 2 minutes. Drain thoroughly and keep warm.

6 Mix the sour cream, mustard, and dill together,

then warm gently. Season to taste with salt and pepper. Divide the spinach among the phyllo pastry nests, and flake the salmon onto the spinach.

7 Spoon the mustard and dill sauce over the phyllo pastry baskets, and serve immediately.

FOOD FACT

This is a highly nutritious dish, combining calcium-rich salmon with vitamin- and mineral-rich spinach. The low-fat sour cream in this recipe can be replaced with low-fat yogurt if you want to aid digestion and give your immune system a real boost!

SMOKED SALMON SUSHI

INGREDIENTS   Serves 4

¾ cup sushi rice
2 tbsp. rice vinegar
4 tsp. sugar
½ tsp salt
2 sheets sushi nori
2½ oz. smoked salmon
¼ cucumber, cut into fine strips

TO SERVE:
wasabi
soy sauce
pickled ginger

1 Rinse the rice thoroughly in cold water until the water runs clear, then place in a large saucepan with 1¼ cups of water. Bring to a boil and cover with a tight-fitting lid. Reduce to a simmer and cook gently for 10 minutes. Turn the heat off, but keep the saucepan covered to allow the rice to steam for an additional 10 minutes.

2 In a small saucepan, gently heat the rice vinegar, sugar, and salt until the sugar has dissolved. When the rice has finished steaming, pour over the vinegar mixture and stir well to mix. Empty the rice out onto a large, flat surface (a chopping board or large plate is ideal). Fan the rice to cool and to produce a shinier rice.

3 Lay one sheet of sushi nori on a sushi mat (if you do not have a sushi mat, improvise with a stiff piece of fabric that is a little larger than the sushi nori), and spread with half the cooled rice. Dampen your hands while doing this, to prevent the rice from sticking to your hands. On the nearest edge, place half the salmon and half the cucumber strips.

4 Roll up the rice and smoked salmon tightly. Dampen the blade of a sharp knife and cut the sushi into slices about ¾ inch thick. Repeat with the remaining sushi nori, rice, smoked salmon, and cucumber. Serve with wasabi, soy sauce, and pickled ginger.

TASTY TIP

If wasabi is unavailable, use a little horseradish. If you cannot find sushi nori (seaweed sheets), shape the rice into small bite-size oblongs, then drape a piece of smoked salmon over each one, and garnish with chives.

HONEY & GINGER SHRIMP

INGREDIENTS
Serves 4

1 carrot
¾ cup bamboo shoots
4 scallions
1 tbsp. honey
1 tbsp. ketchup
1 tsp. soy sauce
1-in. piece fresh ginger, peeled
 and finely grated
1 garlic clove, peeled
 and crushed
1 tbsp. lime juice

6 oz. peeled shrimp, defrosted
 if frozen
2 heads romaine lettuce
2 tbsp. freshly chopped
 cilantro
salt and freshly ground
 black pepper

TO GARNISH:
sprigs of fresh cilantro
lime slices

1 Cut the carrot into matchstick-size pieces, coarsely chop the bamboo shoots, and finely slice the scallions.

2 Combine the bamboo shoots with the carrot matchsticks and scallions.

3 In a wok or large skillet, gently heat the honey, ketchup, soy sauce, ginger, garlic, and lime juice with 3 tablespoons of water. Bring to a boil.

4 Add the carrot mixture and stir-fry for 2–3 minutes until the vegetables are hot.

5 Add the shrimp and continue to stir-fry for 2 minutes.

6 Remove the wok or skillet from the heat, and set aside until cooled slightly.

7 Divide the romaine lettuce into leaves, and rinse lightly under cold running water.

8 Stir the chopped cilantro into the shrimp mixture, and season to taste with salt and pepper. Spoon into the lettuce leaves, and serve immediately, garnished with sprigs of fresh cilantro and lime slices.

HELPFUL HINT

This highly versatile dish can be adapted to suit any diet by increasing and varying the vegetable content. If desired, raw jumbo shrimp can be used for this recipe—make sure that, if using raw shrimp, the black vein that runs along the back is removed.

TUNA CHOWDER

INGREDIENTS   Serves 4

2 tsp. oil
1 onion, peeled and
    finely chopped
2 sticks of celery, trimmed
    and finely sliced
1 tbsp. all-purpose flour
2½ cups nonfat milk
7-oz. can tuna in water

11-oz. can of corn, drained
2 tsp. freshly chopped thyme
salt and freshly ground
    black pepper
pinch of cayenne pepper
2 tbsp. freshly chopped
    parsley

1 Heat the oil in a large, heavy saucepan. Add the onion and celery, and gently cook for about 5 minutes, stirring from time to time until the onion is softened.

2 Stir in the flour and cook for about 1 minute to thicken.

3 Take the saucepan off the heat and gradually pour in the milk, stirring throughout.

4 Add the tuna and its liquid, the drained corn, and the freshly chopped thyme.

5 Mix gently, then bring to a boil. Cover with a lid and simmer for 5 minutes.

6 Remove the saucepan from the heat and season to taste with salt and pepper.

7 Sprinkle the chowder with the cayenne pepper and chopped parsley. Divide among soup bowls and serve immediately.

TASTY TIP

To make this soup even more colorful, use a can of corn with bell peppers. For those who particularly like fish and seafood, add 4 oz. of shelled shrimp for an extra-special flavor.

TASTY TIP

This creamy soup also works well using equivalent amounts of canned crabmeat instead of the tuna.
For a contrasting taste and to enhance the delicate creaminess of this soup, add a spoonful of low-fat sour cream to the top of the soup. Sprinkle with cayenne pepper, and then garnish with a few chopped chives.

ASIAN GROUND CHICKEN ON ARUGULA & TOMATO

INGREDIENTS — Serves 4

2 shallots, peeled	1 tsp. Chinese five spice powder
1 garlic clove, peeled	pinch of chili powder
1 carrot, peeled	1 tsp. soy sauce
½ cup water chestnuts	1 tbsp. fish sauce
1 tsp. oil	8 cherry tomatoes
12 oz. fresh ground chicken	1¼ cups arugula

1 Finely chop the shallots and garlic. Cut the carrot into matchsticks, thinly slice the water chestnuts, and set aside. Heat the oil in a large wok or heavy skillet, and add the chicken. Stir-fry for 3–4 minutes over a moderately high heat, breaking up any large pieces of chicken.

2 Add the garlic and shallots and cook for 2–3 minutes until softened. Sprinkle with the Chinese five spice powder and chili powder, and continue to cook for about 1 minute.

3 Add the carrot, water chestnuts, soy and fish sauce, and 2 tablespoons of water. Stir-fry for an additional 2 minutes. Remove from the heat and set aside to cool slightly.

4 Seed the tomatoes and cut into thin wedges. Toss with the arugula and divide among 4 serving plates. Spoon the warm chicken mixture over the arugula and tomato wedges, and serve immediately to keep the arugula from wilting.

TASTY TIP

This is a very versatile dish. In place of the chicken, you could use any lean cut of meat, or even shrimp. To make this dish a main meal, replace the arugula and tomatoes with stir-fried vegetables and rice. Another alternative that works very well is to serve the chicken mixture in Step 3 in lettuce leaves. Place a spoonful of the mixture into a lettuce leaf and roll up into a small pocket.

GINGERED COD STEAKS

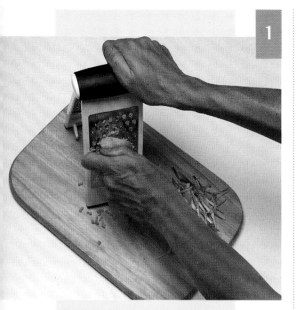

INGREDIENTS   Serves 4

1-in. piece fresh ginger, peeled
4 scallions
2 tsp. freshly chopped parsley
1 tbsp. brown sugar
4 6-oz. cod steaks

salt and freshly ground
   black pepper
¼ stick reduced-fat butter
freshly cooked vegetables,
   to serve

1 Preheat the broiler and line the broiler rack with a layer of foil. Coarsely grate the piece of fresh ginger. Trim the scallions and cut into thin strips.

2 Mix the scallions, ginger, chopped parsley, and sugar together. Add 1 tablespoon of water.

3 Wipe the fish steaks. Season to taste with salt and pepper. Place onto 4 separate 8 x 8 inch foil squares.

4 Carefully spoon the scallions and ginger mixture evenly over the fish.

5 Cut the butter into small cubes and place over the fish.

6 Loosely fold the foil over the steaks to enclose the fish and to make a pocket.

7 Place under the preheated broiler and cook for 10–12 minutes or until cooked and the flesh has turned opaque.

8 Place the fish pockets on individual serving plates. Serve immediately with the freshly cooked vegetables.

HELPFUL HINT

This recipe will also work well with other fish steaks. Try salmon, fresh haddock, or monkfish fillets. The monkfish fillets may take a little longer to cook.

TASTY TIP

Why not serve this dish with roasted new potatoes *en papillote*? Place the new potatoes into double-thickness baking parchment with a few cloves of peeled garlic. Drizzle with a little olive oil and season well with salt and black pepper. Fold all the edges of the waxed paper together, and roast in the preheated oven at 350° F for 40–50 minutes before serving in the paper casing.

SEARED PANCETTA-WRAPPED COD

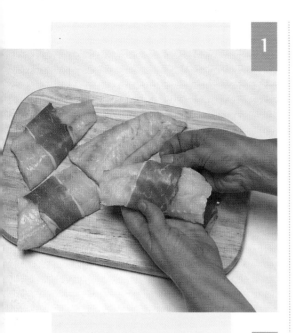

INGREDIENTS   Serves 4

4 6-oz. cod fillets
4 very thin slices of pancetta
3 tbsp. capers, in vinegar
1 tbsp. vegetable or corn oil
2 tbsp. lemon juice
1 tbsp. olive oil
freshly ground black pepper

1 tbsp. freshly chopped
  parsley, to garnish

TO SERVE:
freshly cooked vegetables
new potatoes

1 Wipe the cod fillets and wrap each one with the pancetta. Secure each fillet with a toothpick and set aside.

2 Drain the capers and soak in cold water for 10 minutes to remove any excess salt, then drain and set aside.

3 Heat the oil in a large skillet and sear the wrapped pieces of cod fillet for about 3 minutes on each side, turning carefully with a spatula so as not to break up the fish.

4 Lower the heat, then continue to cook for 2–3 minutes or until the fish is cooked thoroughly.

5 Meanwhile, place the remaining capers, lemon juice, and olive oil in a small saucepan. Add the black pepper.

6 Place the saucepan over a low heat and bring to a gentle simmer, stirring continuously for 2–3 minutes.

7 Once the fish is cooked, garnish with the parsley and serve with the warm caper dressing, freshly cooked vegetables, and new potatoes.

FOOD FACT

Pancetta is Italian-cured belly pork, which is often delicately smoked and sold either finely sliced or chopped coarsely into small cubes. The slices of pancetta can be used to encase poultry and fish, whereas chopped pancetta is often used in sauces. To cook chopped pancetta, fry for 2–3 minutes and set aside. Use the oil to seal meat or to fry onions, then return the pancetta to the pan.

MUSSELS LINGUINE

INGREDIENTS   Serves 4

4½ lbs. fresh mussels, washed
  and scrubbed
pat of butter
1 onion, peeled and
  finely chopped
1¼ cups medium-dry
  white wine

FOR THE SAUCE:
1 tbsp. corn oil
4 baby onions, peeled
  and quartered

2 garlic cloves, peeled
  and crushed
14-oz. can chopped tomatoes
large pinch of salt
3 cups dried linguine
  or tagliatelle
2 tbsp. freshly chopped
  parsley

1 Soak the mussels in plenty of cold water. Leave in the refrigerator until needed. When ready to use, scrub the shells, removing any barnacles or beards. Discard any open mussels.

2 Melt the butter in a large saucepan. Add the mussels, onion, and wine. Cover and steam for 5–6 minutes, shaking the pan gently to ensure even cooking. Discard any mussels that have not opened, then strain and set the liquid aside.

3 To make the sauce, heat the oil in a medium saucepan, and gently cook the quartered onion and garlic for 3–4 minutes until soft and transparent. Stir in the tomatoes and half the set-aside liquid. Bring to a boil, and simmer for 7–10 minutes or until the sauce begins to thicken.

4 Cook the pasta in boiling, salted water for 7 minutes or or until al dente. Drain the pasta, saving 2 tablespoons of the cooking liquid, then return the pasta and liquid to the pan.

5 Remove the meat from half the mussel shells. Stir into the sauce, along with the remaining mussels. Pour the hot sauce over the cooked pasta and toss gently. Garnish with the parsley and serve immediately.

TASTY TIP

Serving mussels in their shells is a fantastic way to eat them. Every mussel is surrounded with the delicious sauce, adding flavor to every mouthful. Clams, which often have a sweeter flavor, could also be used in this recipe.

BARBECUED FISH KABOBS

INGREDIENTS   Serves 4

1 lb. herring or mackerel
   fillets, cut into chunks
2 small red onions, peeled and
   quartered
16 cherry tomatoes
salt and freshly ground
   black pepper
couscous, to serve

FOR THE SAUCE:
⅔ cup fish stock
5 tbsp. ketchup
2 tbsp. Worcestershire sauce
2 tbsp. wine vinegar
2 tbsp. brown sugar
2 drops hot chili sauce
2 tbsp. tomato paste

1 Line a broiler rack with a single layer of foil, and preheat the broiler.

2 If using wooden skewers, soak in cold water for 30 minutes to keep them from burning during cooking.

3 Meanwhile, prepare the sauce. Add the fish stock, ketchup, Worcestershire sauce, vinegar, sugar, hot chili sauce, and tomato paste to a small saucepan. Stir well and leave to simmer for 5 minutes.

4 When ready to cook, drain the skewers, if necessary, then thread the fish chunks, the quartered red onions, and the cherry tomatoes alternately onto the skewers.

5 Season the kabobs to taste with salt and pepper, and brush with the sauce. Broil under the preheated broiler for 8–10 minutes, basting with the sauce occasionally during cooking. Turn the kabobs often to ensure that they are cooked thoroughly and evenly on all sides. Serve immediately with couscous.

TASTY TIP

This dish would be ideal for a light summertime evening meal. Instead of cooking indoors, cook these kabobs on the barbecue for a delicious charcoal flavor. Light the barbecue at least 20 minutes before use in order to allow the coals to heat up. (The coals will have a gray-white ash when ready.) Barbecue some bell peppers and red onions, and serve with a mixed salad as an accompaniment to the fish kabobs.

RATATOUILLE MACKEREL

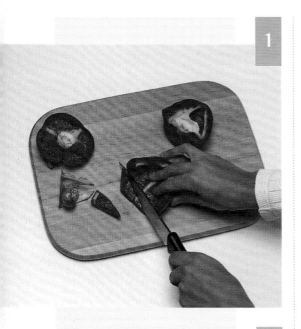

INGREDIENTS

Serves 4

1 red bell pepper
1 tbsp. olive oil
1 red onion, peeled
1 garlic clove, peeled and
  thinly sliced
2 zucchini, trimmed and sliced
14-oz. can chopped tomatoes
sea salt and freshly ground
  black pepper

4 10-oz. small mackerel,
  cleaned and heads removed
spray of olive oil
lemon juice, for drizzling
12 fresh basil leaves
couscous or rice mixed with
  chopped parsley, to serve

1 Preheat the oven to 375° F. Cut the top off the red bell pepper, remove the seeds and membrane, then cut into chunks. Cut the red onion into thick wedges.

2 Heat the oil in a large saucepan, and cook the onion and garlic for 5 minutes or until beginning to soften.

3 Add the bell pepper chunks and zucchini slices, and cook for an additional 5 minutes.

4 Pour in the chopped tomatoes with their juice, and cook for an additional 5 minutes. Season to taste with salt and pepper, and pour into an ovenproof dish.

5 Season the fish with salt and pepper and arrange on top of the vegetables. Spray with a little olive oil and lemon juice. Cover and cook in the preheated oven for 20 minutes.

6 Remove the cover, add the basil leaves, and return to the oven for an additional 5 minutes. Serve immediately with couscous or rice mixed with parsley.

FOOD FACT

Ratatouille is a traditional French dish using onions, tomatoes, zucchini, and often eggplant. It is a very versatile dish to which many other vegetables can be added. For that extra kick, why not add a little chopped chili?

COD WITH FENNEL & CARDAMOM

INGREDIENTS   Serves 4

1 garlic clove, peeled
  and crushed
1 tbsp. grated lemon rind
1 tsp. lemon juice
1 tbsp. olive oil

1 fennel bulb
1 tbsp. cardamom pods
salt and freshly ground
  black pepper
4 6-oz. cod fillets

1 Preheat the oven to 375° F. Place the garlic in a small bowl with the lemon zest, juice, and olive oil, and stir well.

2 Cover with plastic wrap and leave to infuse for at least 30 minutes. Stir well before using.

3 Trim the fennel bulb, thinly slice, and place in a bowl.

4 Place the cardamom pods in a mortar and pestle, and lightly pound to crack the pods.

5 Alternatively, wrap in a piece of plastic wrap and pound gently with a rolling pin. Add the crushed cardamom to the fennel slices.

6 Season the fish with salt and pepper, and place onto 4 separate 8-inch squares of baking parchment.

7 Spoon the fennel mixture over the fish and drizzle with the infused oil, then fold the baking parchment over to enclose the fish and form a pocket.

8 Place the pockets on a baking sheet and cook in the preheated oven for 8–10 minutes or until cooked. Serve immediately in the paper pockets.

FOOD FACT

When buying fresh fish, look for fish that does not smell. Any fish smelling of ammonia should be avoided.
The flesh should be plump and firm-looking. The eyes should be bright, not sunken. If in doubt, choose frozen fish. This is cleaned and packed almost as soon as it is caught. It is often fresher and contains more nutrients than its fresh counterparts.

SEARED TUNA WITH PERNOD & THYME

INGREDIENTS

Serves 4

4 tuna or swordfish steaks
salt and freshly ground
    black pepper
3 tbsp. Pernod
1 tbsp. olive oil
3 tsp. each lime zest and juice

2 tsp. fresh thyme leaves
4 sun-dried tomatoes

TO SERVE:
freshly cooked mixed rice
tossed green salad

1 Wipe the fish steaks with a damp cloth or dampened paper towels.

2 Season both sides of the fish to taste with salt and pepper, then place in a shallow bowl and set aside.

3 Mix together the Pernod, olive oil, lime zest, and juice with the fresh thyme leaves.

4 Finely chop the sun-dried tomatoes, and add to the Pernod mixture.

5 Pour the Pernod mixture over the fish and chill in the refrigerator for about 2 hours, occasionally spooning the marinade over the fish.

6 Heat a griddle or heavy skillet. Drain the fish, setting aside the marinade. Cook the fish for 3–4 minutes on each side for a steak that is still slightly pink in the center. Alternatively, cook the fish for

1–2 minutes longer on each side if you prefer your fish cooked through.

7 Place the remaining marinade in a small saucepan, and bring to a boil. Pour the marinade over the fish, and serve immediately with the mixed rice and salad.

HELPFUL HINT

Tuna is now widely available all year round in supermarkets. Tuna is an oily fish that is rich in omega-3 fatty acids and helps in the prevention of heart disease by lowering blood cholesterol levels. Tuna is usually sold in steaks, and the flesh should be dark red in color.

HADDOCK WITH AN OLIVE CRUST

INGREDIENTS   Serves 4

12 pitted ripe olives,
  finely chopped
¾ cup fresh white
  bread crumbs
1 tbsp. freshly chopped
  tarragon
1 garlic clove, peeled
  and crushed
3 scallions, trimmed and
  finely chopped

1 tbsp. olive oil
4 thick, skinless haddock
  fillets, 6 oz. each

TO SERVE:
freshly cooked carrots
freshly cooked beans

1 Preheat the oven to 375° F. Place the olives in a small bowl with the bread crumbs, and add the chopped tarragon.

2 Add the crushed garlic to the olives with the chopped scallions and the olive oil. Mix together lightly.

3 Wipe the fillets with either a clean, damp cloth or damp paper towels, then place on a lightly greased baking sheet.

4 Place spoonfuls of the olive and bread crumb mixture on top of each fillet, and press the mixture down lightly and evenly over the top of the fish.

5 Bake the fish in the preheated oven for 20–25 minutes or until the fish is cooked thoroughly, and the topping is golden brown. Serve immediately with the freshly cooked carrots and beans.

HELPFUL HINT

Any firm-fleshed fish will be suitable for this delicious and tasty dish. Try substituting cod, monkfish, or even salmon.

TASTY TIP

Why not try experimenting by adding other ingredients to the crust? Adding 2 cloves of roasted garlic gives the crust a delicious flavor. Simply mash the garlic and add to the crumbs. Also, a combination of white and whole-wheat bread crumbs can be used for a nuttier, malty taste.

CITRUS MONKFISH KABOBS

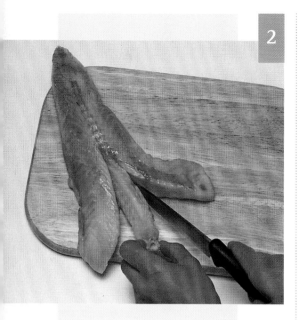

INGREDIENTS   Serves 4

FOR THE MARINADE:
1 tbsp. corn oil
2 tsp. finely grated lime rind
1 tbsp. lime juice
1 tbsp. lemon juice
1 sprig of freshly chopped
    rosemary
1 tbsp. mustard
1 garlic clove, peeled and
    crushed
salt and freshly ground
    black pepper

FOR THE KABOBS:
1 lb. monkfish tail
8 raw jumbo shrimp
1 small green zucchini,
    trimmed and sliced
4 tbsp. low-fat sour cream

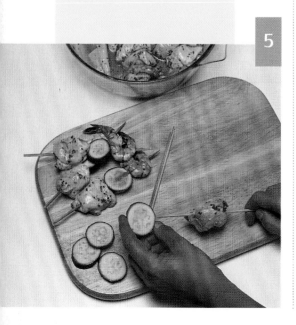

1 Preheat the broiler and line the broiler rack with foil. Mix all the marinade ingredients together in a bowl, and set aside.

2 Using a sharp knife, cut down both sides of the fish tail. Remove the bone and discard. Cut away and discard any skin, then cut the fish into bite-size cubes.

3 Shell the shrimp, leaving the tails intact, and remove the black vein that runs down the back of each. Place the fish and shrimp in a shallow dish.

4 Pour the marinade over the fish and shrimp. Cover lightly and leave to marinate in the refrigerator for 30 minutes. Spoon the marinade over the fish and shrimp occasionally during this time. Soak the skewers in cold water for 30 minutes, then drain.

5 Thread the cubes of fish, shrimp, and zucchini onto the drained skewers.

6 Arrange on the broiler rack, then place under the preheated broiler and cook for 5–7 minutes or until cooked thoroughly and the shrimp have turned pink. Occasionally brush with the remaining marinade, and turn the kabobs during cooking.

7 Mix 2 tablespoons of the marinade with the sour cream and serve as a dip with the kabobs.

FOOD FACT

Monkfish is so versatile—it can be roasted in the oven, poached, baked, or broiled. Its firm flesh is ideal for kabobs.

SARDINES WITH RED CURRANTS

INGREDIENTS
Serves 4

2 tbsp. red currant jelly
2 tsp. finely grated lime rind
2 tbsp. medium-dry sherry
1 lb. fresh sardines, cleaned
    and heads removed
sea salt and freshly ground
    black pepper
lime wedges, to garnish

TO SERVE:
fresh red currants
fresh green salad

1 Preheat the broiler and line the broiler rack with foil 2–3 minutes before cooking.

2 Warm the red currant jelly in a bowl standing over a pan of gently simmering water and stir until smooth. Add the lime rind and sherry to the bowl, and stir until blended.

3 Lightly rinse the sardines and pat dry with absorbent paper towels.

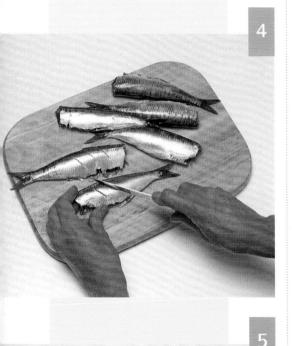

4 Place on a chopping board and with a sharp knife, make several diagonal cuts across the flesh of each fish. Season the sardines inside the cavities with salt and pepper.

5 Gently brush the warm marinade over the skin and inside the cavities of the sardines.

6 Place on the broiler rack and cook under the preheated broiler for 8–10 minutes or until the fish are cooked.

7 Carefully turn the sardines over at least once during broiling. Baste occasionally with the remaining red currant and lime marinade. Garnish with the red currants. Serve immediately with the salad and lime wedges.

COOK'S TIP

Most fish are sold cleaned, but it is easy to do yourself. Using the back of a knife, scrape off the scales from the tail toward the head. Using a sharp knife, make a small slit along the belly. Carefully scrape out the entrails and rinse thoroughly under cold running water. Pat dry with absorbent paper towels.

HOT SALSA-FILLED SOLE

INGREDIENTS   Serves 4

8 6-oz. sole fillets, skinned
⅔ cup orange juice
2 tbsp. lemon juice

FOR THE SALSA:
1 small mango
8 cherry tomatoes, quartered
1 small red onion, peeled
  and finely chopped
pinch of sugar
1 red chili
2 tbsp. rice vinegar

2 tsp. lime zest
1 tbsp. lime juice
1 tbsp. olive oil
sea salt and freshly ground
  black pepper
2 tbsp. freshly chopped mint
lime wedges, to garnish
lettuce leaves, to serve

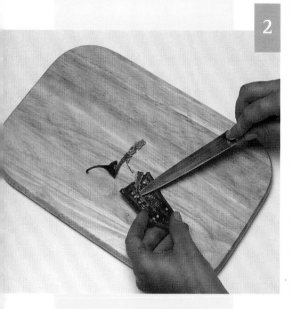

1 First, make the salsa. Peel the mango and cut the flesh away from the pit. Chop finely and place in a small bowl. Add the cherry tomatoes to the mango, along with the onion and sugar.

2 Cut the top of the chili. Slit down the side, and discard the seeds and membrane (the skin to which the seeds are attached). Finely chop the chili and add to the mango mixture with the vinegar, lime zest, juice, and oil. Season to taste with salt and pepper. Mix thoroughly and let stand for 30 minutes to allow the flavors to develop.

3 Lay the fish fillets on a chopping board, skinned-side up, and pile the salsa on the tail end of the fillets. Fold in half, season, and place in a large, shallow skillet. Pour over the orange and lemon juice.

4 Bring to a gentle boil, then reduce the heat to a simmer. Cover and cook on a low heat for 7–10 minutes, adding a little water if the liquid is evaporating. Remove the cover, add the mint, and cook uncovered for an additional 3 minutes. Garnish with lime wedges and serve immediately with the salad.

HELPFUL HINT

Your skin may burn after handling chilies. Take care not to touch your eyes, and wash your hands immediately.

TASTY TIP

To temper the hotness of the salsa, add 1–2 teaspoons of warm honey.

SMOKED HADDOCK RÖSTI

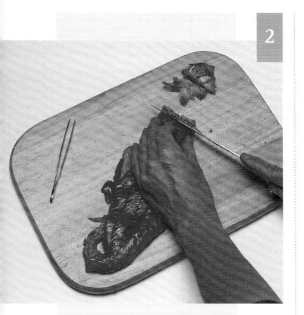

INGREDIENTS — Serves 4

1 lb. potatoes, peeled and
  coarsely grated
1 large onion, peeled and
  coarsely grated
2–3 garlic cloves, peeled
  and crushed
1 lb. smoked haddock
1 tbsp. olive oil

salt and freshly ground
  black pepper
2 tsp. finely grated lemon rind
1 tbsp. freshly chopped
  parsley
2 tbsp. low-fat sour cream
lettuce leaves, to garnish
lemon wedges, to serve

1 Dry the grated potatoes in a clean dishtowel. Rinse the grated onion thoroughly in cold water, dry in a clean dishtowel, and add to the potatoes.

2 Stir the garlic into the potato mixture. Skin the smoked haddock and remove as many of the tiny pin bones as possible. Cut into thin slices and set aside.

3 Heat the oil in a large nonstick skillet. Add half the potatoes and press down in the skillet. Season to taste with salt and pepper.

4 Add a layer of fish and a sprinkling of lemon rind, parsley, and a little black pepper.

5 Top with the remaining potatoes and press down firmly. Cover with a sheet of foil, and cook on the lowest heat for 25–30 minutes.

6 Preheat the broiler 2–3 minutes before the end of the cooking time. Remove the foil and place the rösti under the broiler to brown. Turn out onto a warmed serving dish, and serve immediately with spoonfuls of sour cream, lemon wedges, and mixed lettuce leaves.

HELPFUL HINT

These delicious fish rosti are best if they are prepared, cooked, and then eaten right away.

May 2005 aged

SWEET-&-SOUR SHRIMP WITH NOODLES

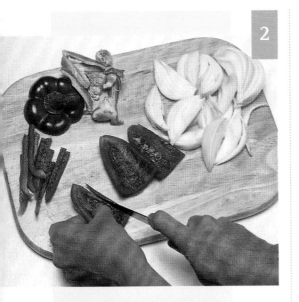

INGREDIENTS   Serves 4

15-oz. can pineapple chunks in
  natural juice
1 green bell pepper, seeded
  and cut into quarters
1 tbsp. peanut oil
1 onion, cut into thin wedges
3 tbsp. brown sugar
⅔ cup chicken stock
4 tbsp. wine vinegar

1 tbsp. tomato paste
1 tbsp. light soy sauce
1 tbsp. cornstarch
12 oz. raw jumbo shrimp,
  shelled
5 cups bok choy, shredded
4¾ cups medium egg noodles
fresh cilantro leaves,
  to garnish

1 Make the sauce by draining the pineapple and setting aside 2 tablespoons of the juice.

2 Remove the membrane from the quartered bell pepper and cut into thin strips.

3 Heat the oil in a saucepan. Add the onion and pepper, and cook for about 4 minutes or until the onion has softened.

4 Add the pineapple, the sugar, stock, vinegar, tomato paste, and the soy sauce.

5 Bring the sauce to a boil and simmer for about 4 minutes. Blend the cornstarch with the pineapple juice and stir into the saucepan, stirring until the sauce has thickened.

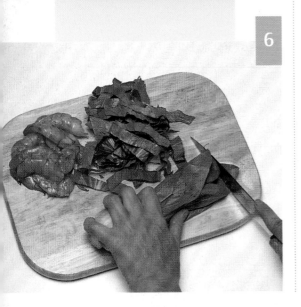

6 Clean the shrimp if necessary. Wash the bok choy thoroughly, then shred.

7 Add the shrimp and bok choy to the sauce. Simmer for 3 minutes or until the shrimp are cooked and have turned pink.

8 Cook the noodles in boiling water for 4–5 minutes until just tender.

9 Drain and arrange the noodles on a warmed serving plate and pour over the shrimp. Garnish with a few cilantro leaves and serve immediately.

HELPFUL HINT

This dish works well with Thai jasmine steamed rice and also whole-wheat noodles, which have more nutritional value. When using raw jumbo shrimp, make sure that the black vein that runs along their backs has been completely removed.

SALMON FISH CAKES

INGREDIENTS   Serves 4

8 oz. potatoes, peeled
1 lb. salmon fillet, skinned
1 medium carrot, trimmed
   and peeled
2 tbsp. grated lemon rind
2–3 tbsp. freshly chopped
   cilantro
1 medium egg yolk
salt and freshly ground
   black pepper

2 tbsp. all-purpose flour
few fine sprays of oil

TO SERVE:
prepared tomato sauce
tossed green salad
crusty bread

1 Cube the potatoes and cook in lightly salted, boiling water for 15 minutes. Drain and mash the potatoes. Place in a large bowl and set aside.

2 Place the salmon in a food processor and blend to form a chunky purée. Add the purée to the potatoes and mix together.

3 Coarsely grate the carrot and add to the fish, along with the lemon rind and the cilantro.

4 Add the egg yolk, season to taste with salt and pepper, then gently mix the ingredients together. With damp hands, form the mixture into 4 large fish cakes.

5 Coat with flour, then place on a plate. Cover loosely and chill for at least 30 minutes.

6 When ready to cook, spray a griddle pan with a few fine sprays of oil and heat the pan. When hot, add the fish cakes and cook on both sides for 3–4 minutes or until the fish is cooked. Add an extra spray of oil if needed during the cooking.

7 When the fish cakes are cooked, serve immediately with the tomato sauce, green salad, and crusty bread.

FOOD FACT

Salmon is now easily affordable due to salmon farming. It is readily available year-round, and is often cheaper to buy than cod. It is an excellent source of omega-3 fatty acids, which help lower blood cholesterol levels.

CITRUS-BROILED FLOUNDER

INGREDIENTS   Serves 4

1 tsp. corn oil
1 onion, peeled and chopped
1 orange bell pepper, seeded
   and chopped
¾ cup long-grain rice
⅔ cup orange juice
2 tbsp. lemon juice
1 cup vegetable stock
spray of oil
4 6-oz. flounder fillets, skinned
1 orange
1 lemon

¼ stick reduced-fat butter
   or 2 tbsp. low-fat spread
2 tbsp. freshly chopped
   tarragon
salt and freshly ground
   black pepper
lemon wedges, to garnish

1 Heat the oil in a large skillet, then cook the onion, bell pepper, and rice for 2 minutes.

2 Add the orange and lemon juice, and bring to a boil. Reduce the heat, add half the stock, and simmer for 15–20 minutes or until the rice is tender, adding the remaining stock as necessary.

3 Preheat the broiler. Finely spray the base of the broiler pan with oil. Place the flounder fillets in the base and set aside.

4 Finely grate the orange and lemon rind. Squeeze the juice from half of each fruit.

5 Melt the butter or low-fat spread in a small saucepan. Add the grated rind, juice, and half of the tarragon, and use to baste the flounder fillets.

6 Cook one side only of the fish under the preheated broiler at a medium heat for 4–6 minutes, basting continuously.

7 Once the rice is cooked, stir in the remaining tarragon, and season to taste with salt and pepper. Garnish the fish with the lemon wedges, and serve immediately with the rice.

TASTY TIP

Flounder is caught mainly in cold Atlantic waters. It can be bought fresh or frozen, whole or in fillets, and can be fried, poached, or broiled. Sole or halibut can be used in place of flounder, but they are more expensive.

FISH LASAGNA

INGREDIENTS   Serves 4

¾ cup mushrooms
1 tsp. vegetable oil
1 onion, peeled and chopped
1 tbsp. freshly chopped
    oregano
14-oz. can chopped tomatoes
1 tbsp. tomato paste
salt and freshly ground
    black pepper
1 lb. cod or haddock fillets,
    skinned
9–12 sheets precooked
    lasagna verde

FOR THE TOPPING:
1 medium egg, beaten
½ cup cottage cheese
½ cup low-fat plain yogurt
½ cup reduced-fat cheddar
    cheese, shredded

TO SERVE:
mixed lettuce leaves
cherry tomatoes

1 Preheat the oven to 375° F.
Wipe the mushrooms, trim
the stalks, and chop. Heat the oil
in a large, heavy saucepan, add
the onion, and gently cook the
onion for 3–5 minutes or until
soft.

2 Stir in the mushrooms, the
oregano, and the chopped
tomatoes with their juice.

3 Blend the tomato paste with
1 tablespoon of water. Stir
into the pan, and season to taste
with salt and pepper.

4 Bring the sauce to a boil,
then simmer uncovered for
5–10 minutes.

5 Remove as many of the tiny
pin bones as possible from
the fish, and cut the fish into

cubes and add to the tomato
sauce mixture. Stir gently and
remove from the heat.

6 Cover the base of an
ovenproof dish with 2–3
sheets of the lasagna verde. Top
with half of the fish mixture.
Repeat the layers, finishing with
the lasagna sheets.

7 To make the topping, mix
together the beaten egg,
cottage cheese, and yogurt. Pour
over the lasagna and sprinkle
with the cheese.

8 Cook the lasagna in the
preheated oven for 40–45
minutes or until the topping is
golden brown and bubbling.
Serve the lasagna immediately
with the mixed lettuce leaves and
cherry tomatoes.

FRUITS DE MER STIR-FRY

INGREDIENTS   Serves 4

1 lb. mixed fresh shellfish,
  such as jumbo shrimp,
  squid, scallops,
  and mussels
1-in. piece fresh ginger
2 garlic cloves, peeled and
  crushed
2 green chilies, seeded and
  finely chopped
3 tbsp. light soy sauce
2 tbsp. olive oil

2 cups baby corn, rinsed
1¾ cups asparagus tips,
  trimmed and cut in half
1 cup snow peas, trimmed
2 tbsp. plum sauce
4 scallions, trimmed and
  shredded, to garnish
freshly cooked rice, to serve

1 Prepare the shellfish. Shell the shrimp, and if necessary, remove the thin black veins from the back of each. Lightly rinse the squid rings and clean the scallops if needed.

2 Remove and discard any mussels that are open. Scrub and debeard the remaining mussels, removing any barnacles from the shells. Cover the mussels with cold water until needed.

3 Peel the fresh ginger and either coarsely grate or shred finely with a sharp knife, and place into a small bowl.

4 Add the garlic and chilies to the small bowl, pour in the soy sauce, and mix well.

5 Place the mixed shellfish, except the mussels, in a bowl and pour over the marinade. Stir, cover, and leave for 15 minutes.

6 Heat a wok until hot, then add the oil and heat until almost smoking. Add the prepared vegetables, stir-fry for 3 minutes, then stir in the plum sauce.

7 Add the shellfish and the mussels with the marinade, and stir-fry for an additional 3–4 minutes or until the fish is cooked. Discard any mussels that have not opened. Garnish with the scallions, and serve immediately with the freshly cooked rice.

HELPFUL HINT

When stir-frying, it is important that the wok is heated before the oil is added. This ensures that the food does not stick to the wok.

ZESTY WHOLE-BAKED FISH

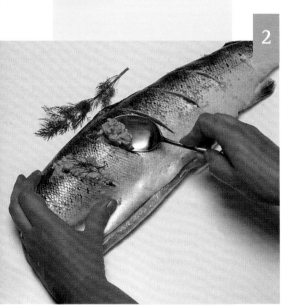

INGREDIENTS   Serves 8

4 lbs. whole salmon, cleaned
sea salt and freshly ground
   black pepper
¼ cup low-fat spread
1 garlic clove, peeled and
   sliced
1 tbsp. lemon zest
1 tbsp. lemon juice
1 tbsp. orange zest
1 tsp. freshly grated nutmeg

3 tbsp. mustard
2 tbsp. fresh, white bread
   crumbs
2 bunches fresh dill
1 bunch fresh tarragon
1 lime, sliced
⅔ cup reduced-fat sour cream
scant 2 cups plain yogurt
sprigs of fresh dill, to garnish

1 Preheat the oven to 425° F. Lightly rinse the fish and pat dry with absorbent paper towels. Season the cavity with a little salt and pepper. Make several diagonal cuts across the flesh of the fish, and season lightly.

2 Mix together the low-fat spread, garlic, lemon, orange zest and juice, nutmeg, mustard, and fresh bread crumbs. Mix well together. Spoon the bread crumb mixture into the slits with a small sprig of dill. Place the remaining herbs inside the fish cavity. Weigh the fish and calculate the cooking time. Allow 10 minutes per pound.

3 Lay the fish on a double thickness of foil. If desired, smear the fish with a little low-fat spread. Top with the lime slices and then fold the foil over to enclose the fish and to form a pocket. Chill in the refrigerator for about 15 minutes.

4 Place in a roasting pan and cook in the preheated oven for the calculated cooking time. Fifteen minutes before the end of cooking, open the foil and return until the skin begins to crisp. Remove the fish from the oven and let stand for 10 minutes.

5 Pour the juices from the roasting pan into a saucepan. Bring to a boil, and stir in the sour cream and yogurt. Simmer for about 3 minutes or until hot. Garnish with dill sprigs and serve immediately.

FOOD FACT

Wild salmon are caught in the freshwaters of North America and Northern Europe. There are many varieties: humpback (pink salmon), chinook, and sockeye. Now that they are farmed, they are more affordable.

SEARED SCALLOP SALAD

INGREDIENTS   Serves 4

12 sea (large) scallops	2 ripe pears, washed
1 tbsp. low-fat spread or butter	2½ cups arugula
2 tbsp. orange juice	2½ cups watercress
2 tbsp. balsamic vinegar	½ cup walnuts
1 tbsp. honey	freshly ground black pepper

1 Clean the scallops, removing the thin black vein from around the white meat and coral. Rinse thoroughly and dry on absorbent paper towels.

2 Cut into 2–3 thick slices, depending on the size of the scallop.

3 Heat a griddle pan or heavy skillet, then when hot, add the low-fat spread or butter, and allow to melt.

4 Once melted, sear the scallops for 1 minute on each side or until golden. Remove from the pan and set aside.

5 Briskly whisk together the orange juice, balsamic vinegar, and honey to make the dressing, and set aside.

6 With a small, sharp knife, carefully cut the pears into quarters, core, and cut into chunks.

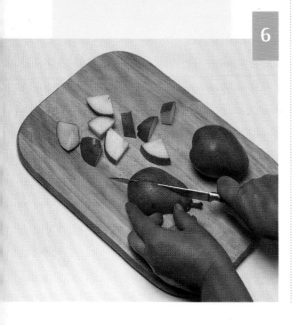

7 Mix the arugula, watercress, pear chunks, and walnuts. Pile onto serving plates and top with the scallops.

8 Drizzle the dressing on top, and add plenty of ground black pepper. Serve immediately.

FOOD FACT

As well as the large sea scallops, which are used in this recipe, there are also the smaller bay scallops. Scallops are in season between September and March, when they will not only be at their best, but they may also be slightly cheaper in price. When buying, especially the larger sea scallops, make sure that the orange coral is left intact.

FISH ROULADES WITH RICE & SPINACH

INGREDIENTS   Serves 4

4 ½-lb. fillets of sole,
  skinned
salt and freshly ground
  black pepper
1 tsp. fennel seeds
1 cup long-grain
  rice, cooked
1 cup white crabmeat, fresh
  or canned

2½ cups baby spinach, washed
  and trimmed
5 tbsp. dry white wine
5 tbsp. reduced-fat sour cream
2 tbsp. freshly chopped
  parsley, plus extra to garnish
asparagus spears, to serve

1 Wipe each fish fillet with either a clean, damp cloth or paper towels. Place on a chopping board, skinned-side up, and season lightly with salt and black pepper.

2 Place the fennel seeds in a mortar and pestle, and crush lightly. Transfer to a small bowl, and stir in the cooked rice. Drain the crabmeat thoroughly. Add to the rice mixture and mix lightly.

3 Lay 2–3 spinach leaves over each fillet, and top with a quarter of the crabmeat mixture. Roll up and secure with a toothpick if necessary. Place into a large saucepan and pour in the wine. Cover and cook for 5–7 minutes or until cooked.

4 Remove the fish from the cooking liquid, and transfer to a serving plate and keep warm. Stir the sour cream into the cooking liquid and season to taste. Heat for 3 minutes, then stir in the chopped parsley.

5 Spoon the sauce onto the base of a plate. Cut each roulade into slices, and arrange on top of the sauce. Serve with freshly cooked asparagus spears.

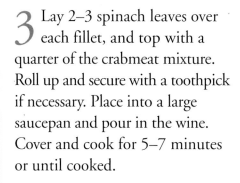

FOOD FACT

Spinach is one of the healthiest leafy green vegetables to be found. It also acts as an antioxidant, and it is believed that it can reduce the risk of certain cancers. Why not use whole-grain rice to add nutritional value and to give the dish a nuttier taste?

CHICKEN WITH ROASTED FENNEL & CITRUS RICE

INGREDIENTS   Serves 4

2 tsp. fennel seeds

1 tbsp. freshly chopped
    oregano

1 garlic clove, peeled and
    crushed

salt and freshly ground
    black pepper

4 chicken quarters, about ½ lb.
    each

½ lemon, finely sliced

1 fennel bulb, trimmed

2 tsp. olive oil

4 plum tomatoes

2 tbsp. pitted green olives

TO GARNISH:

fennel leaves

orange slices

FOR THE CITRUS RICE:

1 cup long-grain rice

2 tsp. finely grated lemon rind

1 tbsp. lemon juice

⅔ cup orange juice

2 cups boiling chicken or
    vegetable stock

1 Preheat the oven to 400° F.
Lightly crush the fennel seeds
and mix with the oregano, garlic,
salt, and pepper. Place between
the skin and flesh of the chicken
breasts, being careful not to tear
the skin. Arrange the lemon slices
on top of the chicken.

2 Cut the fennel into 8 wedges.
Place in a roasting pan with
the chicken. Brush the fennel
with the oil. Cook the chicken
and fennel on the top shelf of the
preheated oven for 10 minutes.

3 Meanwhile, put the rice in a
large ovenproof dish. Stir in
the lemon rind and juice, orange
juice, and stock. Cover with a
tight-fitting lid and put on the
center shelf of the oven.

4 Reduce the oven temperature
to 350° F. Cook the chicken
for an additional 40 minutes,
turning the fennel wedges and
lemon slices once. Seed and chop
the tomatoes. Add to the tray and
cook for 5–10 minutes. Remove
from the oven.

5 When cooled slightly, remove
the chicken skin and discard.
Fluff the rice, then sprinkle with
olives. Garnish with fennel leaves
and orange slices, and serve.

HELPFUL HINT

Check that the chicken is
cooked thoroughly by piercing
the thickest part with a skewer.
The juices should run clear.

BRAISED CHICKEN IN BEER

INGREDIENTS   Serves 4

4 chicken joints, skinned
⅔ cup pitted dried prunes
2 bay leaves
12 shallots
2 tsp. olive oil
1¾ cups small button
   mushrooms, wiped
1 tsp. dark brown sugar
½ tsp. mustard
2 tsp. tomato paste
⅔ cup light beer

⅔ cup chicken stock
salt and freshly ground
   black pepper
2 tsp. cornstarch
2 tsp. lemon juice
2 tbsp. freshly chopped parsley
Italian parsley, to garnish

TO SERVE:
mashed potatoes
seasonal green vegetables

1 Preheat the oven to 325° F. Cut each chicken joint in half and put in an ovenproof casserole dish with the prunes and bay leaves.

2 To peel the shallots, put in a small bowl and cover with boiling water.

3 After 2 minutes, drain the shallots and rinse under cold water until cool enough to handle. The skins should then peel away easily from the shallots.

4 Heat the oil in a large nonstick skillet. Add the shallots and cook gently for about 5 minutes until beginning to brown.

5 Add the mushrooms to the skillet and cook for an additional 3–4 minutes until both the mushrooms and onions are softened.

6 Sprinkle the sugar over the shallots and mushrooms, then add the mustard, tomato paste, beer, and chicken stock. Season to taste with salt and pepper, and bring to a boil, stirring to combine. Carefully pour over the chicken.

7 Cover the casserole and cook in the preheated oven for 1 hour. Blend the cornstarch with the lemon juice and 1 tablespoon of cold water, and stir into the chicken casserole.

8 Return to the oven for an additional 10 minutes or until the chicken is cooked and the vegetables are tender.

9 Remove the bay leaves and stir in the chopped parsley. Garnish the chicken with the Italian parsley. Serve with the mashed potatoes and fresh green vegetables.

CHICKEN BAKED IN A SALT CRUST

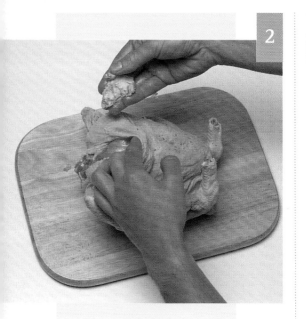

INGREDIENTS   Serves 4

4-lb. oven-ready chicken
salt and freshly ground
　　black pepper
1 medium onion, peeled
sprig of fresh rosemary
sprig of fresh thyme
1 bay leaf
1 tbsp. butter, softened
1 garlic clove, peeled and
　　crushed
pinch of paprika
2 tsp. finely grated lemon rind

TO GARNISH:
fresh herbs
lemon slices

FOR THE SALT CRUST:
8 cups all-purpose flour
3⅔ cups fine cooking salt
3⅔ cups coarse sea salt
2 tbsp. oil

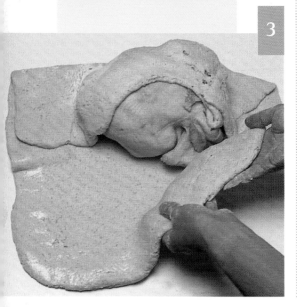

1 Preheat the oven to 325° F. Remove the giblets if necessary, and rinse the chicken with cold water. Sprinkle the inside with salt and pepper. Put the onion inside, along with with the rosemary, thyme, and bay leaf.

2 Mix the butter, garlic, paprika, and lemon rind together. Starting at the neck end, gently ease the skin from the chicken and push the mixture under.

3 To make the salt crust, put the flour and salts in a large bowl, and stir together. Make a well in the center. Pour in 2 cups of cold water and the oil. Mix to a stiff dough, then knead on a lightly floured surface for 2–3 minutes. Roll out the dough to a 20-inch circle. Place the chicken breast-side down in the center. Lightly brush the edges with water, then fold over to enclose. Pinch the joints together to seal.

4 Put the chicken joint-side down in a roasting pan, and cook in the preheated oven for 2¾ hours. Remove from the oven and let stand for 20 minutes.

5 Break open the hard crust and remove the chicken. Discard the crust. Remove the skin from the chicken, and garnish with the fresh herbs and lemon slices. Serve the chicken immediately.

HELPFUL HINT

It is best to avoid eating the skin from the chicken. It is high in fat and absorbs a lot of salt from the crust.

SPICY CHICKEN SKEWERS WITH MANGO TABBOULEH

INGREDIENTS   Serves 4

¾ lb. chicken breast fillet
1 cup low-fat plain yogurt
1 garlic clove, peeled and
   crushed
1 small red chili, seeded and
   finely chopped
½ tsp. turmeric
2 tsp. finely grated lemon rind
2 tsp. lemon juice
sprigs of fresh mint, to garnish

FOR THE TABBOULEH:
1 cup bulgur
1 tsp. olive oil
1 tbsp. lemon juice
½ red onion, finely chopped
1 ripe mango, halved, pitted,
   peeled, and chopped
¼ cucumber, finely diced
2 tbsp. freshly chopped parsley
2 tbsp. freshly torn mint
salt and finely ground
   black pepper

1 If using wooden skewers, presoak them in cold water for 30 minutes. This keeps them from burning during broiling.

2 Cut the chicken into 2 x ½ inch strips, and place in a shallow dish.

3 Mix together the yogurt, garlic, chili, turmeric, lemon rind, and juice. Pour over the chicken and toss to coat. Cover and leave to marinate in the refrigerator for up to 8 hours.

4 To make the tabbouleh, put the bulgur in a bowl. Pour in enough boiling water to cover. Put a plate over the bowl. Allow to soak for 20 minutes.

5 Whisk together the oil and lemon juice in a bowl. Add the red onion and leave to marinate for 10 minutes.

6 Drain the bulgur and squeeze out any excess moisture in a clean dishtowel. Add to the red onion with the mango, cucumber, herbs, and season to taste with salt and pepper. Toss together to mix thoroughly.

7 Thread the chicken strips onto 8 wooden or metal skewers. Cook under a hot broiler for 8 minutes. Turn and brush with the marinade until the chicken is lightly browned and cooked through.

8 Spoon the tabbouleh onto individual plates. Arrange the chicken skewers on top, and garnish with the sprigs of mint. Serve warm or cold.

PAN-COOKED CHICKEN WITH THAI SPICES

INGREDIENTS   Serves 4

4 kaffir lime leaves
2-in. piece fresh ginger, peeled
   and chopped
1¼ cups chicken stock, boiling
4 ½-lb. chicken breasts
2 tsp. peanut oil
5 tbsp. coconut milk
1 tbsp. fish sauce
2 red chilies, seeded and
   finely chopped
1 cup Thai jasmine rice
1 tbsp. lime juice

3 tbsp. freshly chopped
   cilantro
salt and freshly ground
   black pepper

TO GARNISH:
lime wedges
freshly chopped cilantro

1 Lightly bruise the kaffir lime leaves and put in a bowl with the chopped ginger. Pour in the chicken stock, cover, and allow to infuse for 30 minutes.

2 Meanwhile, cut each chicken breast into 2 pieces. Heat the oil in a large nonstick skillet or flameproof casserole dish, and brown the chicken pieces for 2–3 minutes on each side.

3 Strain the infused chicken stock into the skillet. Half-cover the skillet with a lid, and gently simmer for 10 minutes.

4 Stir in the coconut milk, fish sauce, and chopped chilies. Simmer uncovered for 5–6 minutes or until the chicken is tender and cooked through, and the sauce has reduced slightly.

5 Meanwhile, cook the rice in boiling, salted water according to the package instructions. Drain the rice thoroughly.

6 Stir the lime juice and chopped cilantro into the sauce. Season to taste with salt and pepper. Serve the dish on a bed of rice. Garnish with wedges of lime and freshly chopped cilantro and serve immediately.

FOOD FACT

Fresh kaffir lime leaves can be found in Asian food stores. Most supermarkets now stock dried kaffir lime leaves. If using dried, crumble lightly and use as above.

Sauvignon Chicken & Mushroom Phyllo Pie

INGREDIENTS   Serves 4

1 onion, peeled and chopped
1 leek, trimmed and chopped
1 cup chicken stock
1 ½ lbs. chicken breast
⅔ cup dry white wine
1 bay leaf
2½ cups button mushrooms
2 tbsp. all-purpose flour
1 tbsp. freshly chopped
  tarragon

salt and freshly ground
  black pepper
sprig of fresh parsley,
  to garnish
seasonal vegetables, to serve

TOPPING:
5–6 sheets phyllo pastry
1 tbsp. corn oil
1 tsp. sesame seeds

1 Preheat the oven to 375° F. Put the chopped onion and leek in a heavy saucepan with ½ cup of the stock.

2 Bring to a boil, cover, and simmer for 5 minutes, then uncover and cook until all the stock has evaporated, and the vegetables are tender.

3 Cut the chicken into bite-size cubes. Add to the saucepan with the remaining stock, wine, and bay leaf. Cover and gently simmer for about 5 minutes. Add the baby button mushrooms, and simmer for an additional 5 minutes.

4 Blend the flour with 3 tablespoons of cold water. Stir into the saucepan and cook, stirring all the time, until the sauce has thickened.

5 Stir the tarragon into the sauce, and season to taste with salt and pepper.

6 Spoon the mixture into a large, deep pie plate, discarding the bay leaf.

7 Brush a sheet of phyllo pastry with a little of the oil.

8 Crumple the pastry slightly. Arrange on top of the filling. Repeat with the remaining phyllo sheets and oil, then sprinkle the top of the pie with the sesame seeds.

9 Cook the pie on the center shelf of the preheated oven for 20 minutes until the phyllo pastry topping is golden and crisp. Garnish with a sprig of parsley. Serve the pie immediately with the seasonal vegetables.

CHILI ROAST CHICKEN

INGREDIENTS

Serves 4

3 medium-hot, fresh red
   chilies, seeded
½ tsp. turmeric
1 tsp. cumin seeds
1 tsp. coriander seeds
2 garlic cloves, peeled and
   crushed
1-in. piece fresh ginger, peeled
   and chopped
1 tbsp. lemon juice
1 tbsp. olive oil
2 tbsp. coarsely chopped
   fresh cilantro

½ tsp. salt
freshly ground black pepper
3 lbs. oven-ready chicken
1 tbsp. unsalted butter, melted
1¼ lbs. butternut squash
sprigs of fresh parsley and
   cilantro, to garnish

TO SERVE:
4 baked potatoes
seasonal green vegetables

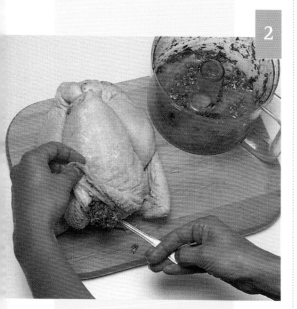

1 Preheat the oven to 375° F. Coarsely chop the chilies, and put in a food processor with the turmeric, cumin seeds, coriander seeds, garlic, ginger, lemon juice, olive oil, cilantro, salt, pepper, and 2 tablespoons of cold water. Blend to a paste, leaving the ingredients still slightly chunky.

2 Starting at the neck end of the chicken, gently ease up the skin to loosen it from the breast. Set aside 3 tablespoons of the paste. Push the remaining paste over the chicken breast, spreading it evenly under the skin.

3 Put the chicken in a large roasting pan. Mix the chili paste with the melted butter. Use 1 tablespoon to brush evenly over the chicken. Roast in the oven for 20 minutes.

4 Meanwhile, halve, peel, and scoop out the seeds from the butternut squash. Cut into large chunks, and mix in the remaining chili paste and butter mixture.

5 Arrange the butternut squash around the chicken. Roast for an additional hour, basting with the cooking juices about every 20 minutes until the chicken is fully cooked and the squash is tender. Garnish with parsley and cilantro. Serve hot with baked potatoes and green vegetables.

HELPFUL HINT

Chilies vary considerably in heat. A good guide is the smaller the chili, the hotter it is. Red chilies are sweeter than green ones.

AROMATIC CHICKEN CURRY

INGREDIENTS   Serves 4

⅔ cup red lentils
2 tsp. ground coriander
½ tsp. cumin seeds
2 tsp. mild curry paste
1 bay leaf
small strip of lemon rind
2½ cups chicken or
  vegetable stock
8 chicken thighs, skinned
¾ cup spinach leaves, rinsed
  and shredded

1 tbsp. freshly chopped
  cilantro
2 tsp. lemon juice
salt and freshly ground
  black pepper

TO SERVE:
freshly cooked rice
low-fat plain yogurt

1 Put the lentils in a sieve and rinse thoroughly under cold running water.

2 Fry the ground coriander and cumin seeds in a large saucepan over a low heat for about 30 seconds. Stir in the curry paste.

3 Add the lentils to the saucepan with the bay leaf and lemon rind, then pour in the stock.

4 Stir, then slowly bring to a boil. Turn down the heat, half-cover the saucepan with a lid, and simmer gently for 5 minutes, stirring occasionally.

5 Secure the chicken thighs with toothpicks to hold their shape. Place in the saucepan and half-cover. Simmer for 15 minutes.

6 Stir in the shredded spinach, and cook for an additional

25 minutes or until the chicken is very tender, and the sauce is thick.

7 Remove the bay leaf and lemon rind. Stir in the cilantro and lemon juice, then season to taste with salt and pepper. Serve immediately with the rice and some plain yogurt.

HELPFUL HINT

Frying spices really releases the flavor of the spices and is a technique that can be used in many dishes. It is a particularly good way to flavor lean meat or fish. Try mixing fried spices with a little water or oil to make a paste. Spread the paste on meat or fish before cooking to make a spicy crust.

CHEESY CHICKEN BURGERS

INGREDIENTS   Serves 6

1 tbsp. corn oil

1 small onion, peeled and
  finely chopped

1 garlic clove, peeled and
  crushed

½ red bell pepper, seeded and
  finely chopped

1 lb. fresh ground chicken

2 tbsp. nonfat plain yogurt

½ cup whole-wheat bread
  crumbs

1 tbsp. freshly chopped herbs,
  such as parsley or tarragon

½ cup cheddar cheese,
  crumbled

salt and freshly ground
  black pepper

**FOR THE CORN AND
  CARROT RELISH:**

7-oz. can corn, drained

1 carrot, peeled, and grated

½ green chili, seeded and
  finely chopped

2 tsp. cider vinegar

2 tsp. light brown sugar

TO SERVE:

whole-wheat rolls

lettuce

sliced tomatoes

mixed lettuce leaves

1 Preheat the broiler. Heat the oil in a skillet and gently cook the onion and garlic for 5 minutes. Add the red bell pepper and cook for 5 minutes. Transfer into a bowl and set aside.

2 Add the chicken, yogurt, bread crumbs, herbs, and cheese, and season to taste with salt and pepper. Mix well.

3 Divide and shape the mixture into 6 burgers. Cover and chill in the refrigerator for at least 20 minutes.

4 To make the relish, put all the ingredients in a small saucepan with 1 tablespoon of water, and heat gently, stirring occasionally, until all the sugar has dissolved.

5 Cover and cook over a low heat for 2 minutes, then uncover and cook for an additional minute or until the relish is thick.

6 Place the burgers on a lightly greased broiler pan, and broil under a medium heat for 8–10 minutes on each side or until browned and cooked through.

7 Warm the rolls, if desired, then split in half and fill with the burgers, lettuce, sliced tomatoes, and relish.

CHICKEN CACCIATORE

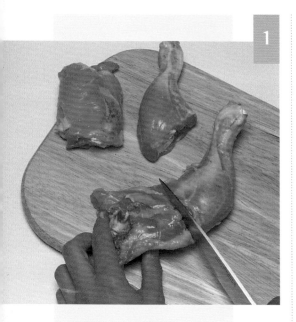

INGREDIENTS   Serves 4

4 chicken legs
1 tbsp. olive oil
1 red onion, peeled and cut
   into very thin wedges
1 garlic clove, peeled and
   crushed
sprig of fresh thyme
sprig of fresh rosemary
⅔ cup dry white wine
1 cup chicken stock

14-oz. can chopped tomatoes
¼ cup pitted ripe olives,
2 tbsp. capers, drained
salt and freshly ground
   black pepper
freshly cooked fettuccine,
   linguine, or pasta shells

1 Skin the chicken pieces and cut each one into 2 pieces to make 4 thighs and 4 drumsticks.

2 Heat 2 teaspoons of the oil in a flameproof casserole dish and cook the chicken for 2–3 minutes on each side until lightly browned. Remove the chicken from the dish and set aside.

3 Add the remaining 1 teaspoon of oil to the juices in the dish.

4 Add the red onion and gently cook for 5 minutes, stirring occasionally.

5 Add the garlic and cook for an additional 5 minutes until soft and beginning to brown. Return the chicken to the casserole dish.

6 Add the herbs, then pour in the wine, and let it boil for 1–2 minutes.

7 Add the stock and tomatoes, cover, and gently simmer for 15 minutes.

8 Stir in the olives and capers. Cook uncovered for an additional 5 minutes or until the chicken is cooked and the sauce is thickened. Remove the herbs and season to taste with salt and pepper.

9 Place the chicken on a bed of pasta, allowing 1 thigh and 1 drumstick per person. Spoon the sauce on top, and serve.

HELPFUL HINT

When watching your saturated fat intake, it is essential to remove the skin from the chicken before eating. Any fat is deposited directly underneath the skin.

CHICKEN & SUMMER VEGETABLE RISOTTO

INGREDIENTS

Serves 4

4 cups chicken or vegetable stock

1¼ cups baby asparagus spears

¾ cup fine green beans

1 tbsp. butter

1 small onion, peeled and finely chopped

⅔ cup dry white wine

1¼ cups risotto rice

pinch of saffron strands

¾ cup frozen peas, defrosted

2½ cups cooked chicken, skinned and diced

1-2 tbsp. lemon juice

salt and freshly ground black pepper

¼ cup Parmesan cheese, shaved

1 Bring the stock to a boil in a large saucepan. Trim the asparagus and cut into 1½-inch lengths.

2 Blanch the asparagus in the stock for 1–2 minutes or until tender, then remove with a slotted spoon, and set aside.

3 Halve the fine green beans and cook in the boiling stock for 4 minutes. Remove and set aside. Turn down the heat and keep the stock barely simmering.

4 Melt the butter in a heavy saucepan. Add the onion and cook gently for about 5 minutes.

5 Pour the wine into the saucepan and boil rapidly until the liquid has almost reduced. Add the rice and cook, stirring, for 1 minute until the grains are coated and look translucent.

6 Add the saffron and a ladle of the stock. Simmer, stirring all the time, until the stock has been absorbed. Continue adding the stock, a ladle at a time, until it is all absorbed.

7 After 15 minutes, the risotto should be creamy with a slight bite to it. If not, add a little more stock and cook for a few more minutes or until it is of the correct texture and consistency.

8 Add the peas, the remaining vegetables, chicken, and lemon juice. Season to taste with salt and pepper, and cook for 3-4 minutes or until the chicken is heated thoroughly and piping hot.

9 Spoon the risotto onto warmed serving plates. Sprinkle each portion with a few shavings of Parmesan cheese and serve immediately.

MEXICAN CHICKEN

INGREDIENTS

Serves 4

3 lbs. oven-ready chicken, jointed
3 tbsp. all-purpose flour
½ tsp. paprika
salt and freshly ground black pepper
2 tsp. corn oil
1 small onion, peeled and chopped
1 red chili, seeded and finely chopped
½ tsp. ground cumin
½ tsp. dried oregano
1¼ cups chicken or vegetable stock

1 green bell pepper, seeded and sliced
2 tsp. cocoa
1 tbsp. lime juice
2 tsp. honey
3 tbsp. nonfat plain yogurt

TO GARNISH:
sliced limes
red chili slices
sprig of fresh oregano

TO SERVE:
freshly cooked rice
fresh green lettuce leaves

1 Using a knife, remove the skin from the chicken joints.

2 In a shallow dish, mix together the flour, paprika, salt, and pepper. Coat the chicken on both sides with flour, and shake off any excess if necessary.

3 Heat the oil in a large nonstick skillet. Add the chicken and brown on both sides. Transfer to a plate and set aside.

4 Add the onion and red chili to the skillet, and gently cook for 5 minutes or until the onion is soft. Stir occasionally.

5 Stir in the cumin and oregano, and cook for an additional minute. Pour in the stock and bring to a boil.

6 Return the chicken to the skillet, cover, and cook for 40 minutes. Add the green bell pepper and cook for 10 minutes until the chicken is cooked. Using a slotted spoon, remove the chicken and pepper, and keep warm in a serving dish.

7 Blend the cocoa with 1 tablespoon of warm water. Stir into the sauce, then boil rapidly until the sauce has thickened and reduced by about one-third. Stir in the lime juice, honey, and yogurt.

8 Pour the sauce over the chicken and pepper, and garnish with the lime slices, chili, and oregano. Serve immediately with the freshly cooked rice and green salad.

TURKEY & TOMATO TAGINE

INGREDIENTS

Serves 4

FOR THE MEATBALLS:

1 lb. fresh ground turkey

1 small onion, peeled and
  very finely chopped

1 garlic clove, peeled and
  crushed

1 tbsp. freshly chopped
  cilantro

1 tsp. cumin

1 tbsp. olive oil

salt and freshly ground
  black pepper

FOR THE SAUCE:

1 onion, peeled and finely
  chopped

1 garlic clove, peeled and
  crushed

⅔ cup turkey stock

14-oz. can chopped tomatoes

½ tsp. ground cumin

½ tsp. ground cinnamon

pinch of cayenne pepper

freshly chopped parsley

freshly chopped herbs,
  to garnish

couscous or rice, to serve

1 Preheat the oven to 375° F. Put all the ingredients (except for the oil) for the meatballs in a bowl, and mix well. Season to taste with salt and pepper. Shape into 20 balls, about the size of walnuts.

2 Put on a tray, cover lightly, and chill in the refrigerator while making the sauce.

3 Put the onion and garlic in a saucepan with ½ cup of the stock. Cook over a low heat until all the stock has evaporated. Continue cooking for 1 minute or until the onions start to brown.

4 Add the remaining stock to the pan with the tomatoes, cumin, cinnamon, and cayenne pepper. Simmer for 10 minutes until slightly thickened and reduced. Stir in the parsley and season to taste.

5 Heat the oil in a large nonstick skillet, and cook the meatballs in 2 batches until lightly browned all over.

6 Using a slotted spoon, lift the meatballs out, and drain on absorbent paper towels.

7 Pour the sauce into a tagine or an ovenproof casserole dish. Top with the meatballs, cover, and cook in the preheated oven for 25–30 minutes or until the meatballs are cooked through and the sauce is bubbling. Garnish with freshly chopped herbs, and serve immediately with couscous or plain boiled rice.

TURKEY ESCALOPES WITH APRICOT CHUTNEY

INGREDIENTS

Serves 4

4 turkey steaks, ¼ lb. each
1 tbsp. all-purpose flour
salt and freshly ground
  black pepper
1 tbsp. olive oil
sprigs of Italian parsley,
  to garnish
orange wedges, to serve

FOR THE APRICOT CHUTNEY:

⅔ cup dried apricots, chopped
1 red onion, peeled and
  finely chopped
1 tsp. freshly grated ginger
2 tbsp. sugar
½ tbsp. grated orange rind
½ cup fresh orange juice
½ cup ruby port
1 whole clove
1 tbsp. freshly chopped
  cilantro

1 Put a turkey steak onto a sheet of plastic wrap or nonstick baking parchment. Cover with a second sheet.

2 Using a rolling pin, gently pound the turkey until the meat is flattened to about ¼ inch thick. Repeat to make 4 escalopes.

3 Mix the flour with the salt and pepper, and use to lightly dust the turkey escalopes.

4 Put the turkey escalopes on a board or cookie sheet, and cover with a piece of plastic wrap or nonstick baking parchment. Chill in the refrigerator until ready to cook.

5 For the apricot chutney, put the apricots, onion, ginger, sugar, orange rind, orange juice, port, and clove into a saucepan.

6 Slowly bring to a boil and simmer uncovered for 10 minutes, stirring occasionally, until thick and syrupy.

7 Remove the clove and stir in the chopped cilantro.

8 Heat the oil in a griddle pan, and cook the turkey escalopes (in 2 batches if necessary) for 3–4 minutes on each side until golden brown and tender.

9 Spoon the chutney onto 4 individual serving plates. Place a turkey escalope on top of each spoonful of chutney. Garnish with sprigs of parsley, and serve immediately with orange wedges.

SMOKED TURKEY TAGLIATELLE

INGREDIENTS   Serves 4

2 tsp. olive oil

1 bunch scallions, trimmed
  and diagonally sliced

1 garlic clove, peeled and
  crushed

1 small zucchini, trimmed,
  sliced, and cut in half

4 tbsp. dry white wine

14-oz. can chopped tomatoes

2 tbsp. freshly torn basil

salt and freshly ground
  black pepper

2 cups spinach and egg
  tagliatelle

¼ lb. smoked turkey breast, cut
  into strips

small fresh basil leaves,
  to garnish

1 Heat the oil in a large saucepan. Add the scallions and garlic, and gently cook for 2–3 minutes until beginning to soften. Stir in the sliced zucchini and cook for 1 minute.

2 Add the wine and let it boil for 1–2 minutes. Stir in the chopped tomatoes, bring to a boil, and simmer, uncovered, over a low heat for 15 minutes or until the zucchini is tender and the sauce slightly reduced. Stir the shredded basil into the sauce, and season to taste with salt and pepper.

3 Meanwhile, bring a large saucepan of salted water to a boil. Add the tagliatelle and cook for 10 minutes until al dente, or according to the package instructions. Drain thoroughly.

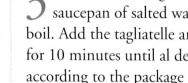

4 Return the tagliatelle to the saucepan, add half the tomato sauce, and toss together to coat the pasta thoroughly in the sauce. Cover and set aside.

5 Add the strips of turkey to the remaining sauce and heat gently for 2–3 minutes until piping hot.

6 Divide the tagliatelle among 4 serving plates. Spoon the sauce on top, garnish with basil leaves, and serve immediately.

TASTY TIP

Many stores and supermarkets now stock flavored pasta, as well as the plain traditional type. Why not try using a garlic and herb or sun-dried tomato tagliatelle in this recipe?

Turkey & Mixed Mushroom Lasagna

INGREDIENTS   Serves 4

1 tbsp. olive oil
2 cups mixed mushrooms,
    such as button, chestnut,
    and portobello, wiped
    and sliced
1 tbsp. butter
¼ cup all-purpose flour
1¼ cups nonfat milk
1 bay leaf
2½ cups cooked turkey, cubed
¼ tsp. freshly grated nutmeg
salt and freshly ground
    black pepper

14-oz. can plum tomatoes,
    drained and chopped
1 tsp. dried mixed herbs
9 lasagna sheets

FOR THE TOPPING:
1 cup nonfat plain yogurt
1 medium egg, lightly beaten
1 tbsp. finely shredded
    Parmesan cheese
mixed lettuce leaves, to serve

1 Preheat the oven to 350° F. Heat the oil and cook the mushrooms until tender and the juices have evaporated. Remove and set aside.

2 Put the butter, flour, milk, and bay leaf in the saucepan. Slowly bring to a boil, stirring until thickened. Simmer for 2–3 minutes. Remove the bay leaf, and stir in the mushrooms, turkey, nutmeg, salt, and pepper.

3 Mix together the tomatoes and mixed herbs, and season with salt and pepper. Spoon half into the base of a large ovenproof dish. Top with 3 sheets of lasagna, then with half the turkey mixture. Repeat the layers, then arrange the remaining 3 sheets of pasta on top.

4 Mix together the yogurt and egg. Spoon over the lasagna, spreading the mixture into the corners. Sprinkle with the Parmesan, and cook in the preheated oven for 45 minutes. Serve with the mixed salad.

TASTY TIP

Garlic bread is the perfect accompaniment to lasagna. Preheat the oven to 350° F. Finely chop 2–3 garlic cloves. Mix with a little chopped parsley and ½ cup of low-fat spread. Make cuts almost to the base of a loaf of French bread. Spread with the flavored, low-fat spread. Wrap in foil. Cook in the preheated oven for 15 minutes.

Teriyaki Turkey with Asian Vegetables

INGREDIENTS   Serves 4

1 red chili
1 garlic clove, peeled and
  crushed
1-in. piece ginger, peeled and
  grated
3 tbsp. dark soy sauce
1 tsp. corn oil
¾ lb. skinless, boneless turkey
  breast
1 tbsp. vegetable oil
1 tbsp. sesame seeds
2 carrots, peeled and cut
into matchsticks

1 leek, trimmed and shredded
1¼ cups broccoli, cut into
  tiny florets
1 tsp. cornstarch
3 tbsp. dry sherry
1 cup snow peas, cut into
  thin strips

TO SERVE:

freshly cooked egg noodles
sprinkling of sesame seeds

1 Halve, seed, and thinly slice the chili. Put into a small bowl with the garlic, ginger, soy sauce, and corn oil.

2 Cut the turkey into thin strips. Add to the mixture and mix until well coated. Cover with plastic wrap and marinate in the refrigerator for at least 30 minutes.

3 Heat a wok or large skillet. Add 2 teaspoons of the vegetable oil. When hot, remove the turkey from the marinade. Stir-fry for 2–3 minutes until browned and cooked. Remove from the wok and set aside.

4 Heat the remaining 1 teaspoon of oil in the wok. Add the sesame seeds and stir-fry for a few seconds until they start to brown.

5 Add the carrots, leek, and broccoli, and continue stir-frying for 2–3 minutes.

6 Blend the cornstarch with 1 tablespoon of cold water to make a smooth paste. Stir in the sherry and marinade. Add to the wok with the snow peas, and cook for 1 minute, stirring all the time, until thickened.

7 Return the turkey to the wok and continue cooking for 1–2 minutes or until the turkey is hot, the vegetables are tender, and the sauce is bubbling. Serve the turkey and vegetables immediately with the egg noodles. Sprinkle with the sesame seeds.

GAME HEN WITH CALVADOS & APPLES

INGREDIENTS

Serves 4

4 game hen breasts, each
  about ¼ lb., skinned
1 tbsp. all-purpose flour
1 tbsp. corn oil
1 onion, peeled and finely
  sliced
1 garlic clove, peeled and
  crushed
1 tsp. freshly chopped thyme
⅔ cup dry cider

salt and freshly ground
  black pepper
3 tbsp. Calvados brandy
sprigs of fresh thyme,
  to garnish

CARAMELIZED APPLES:
1 tbsp. unsalted butter
2 red-skinned apples,
  quartered, cored, and sliced
1 tsp. sugar

1 Lightly dust the game hen breasts with the flour.

2 Heat 2 teaspoons of the oil in a large nonstick skillet and cook the breasts for 2–3 minutes on each side until browned. Remove the breasts from the skillet and set aside.

3 Heat the remaining teaspoon of oil in the skillet, and add the onion and garlic. Cook over a medium heat for 10 minutes, stirring occasionally, until soft and just beginning to brown.

4 Stir in the chopped thyme and cider. Return the game hens to the skillet, season with salt and pepper, and bring to a very gentle simmer. Cover and cook over a low heat for 15–20 minutes or until the game hens are tender.

5 Remove the game hens and keep warm. Turn up the heat and boil the sauce until thickened and reduced by half.

6 Meanwhile, prepare the caramelized apples. Melt the butter in a small nonstick saucepan, add the apple slices in a single layer, and sprinkle with the sugar. Cook until the apples are tender and beginning to caramelize, turning once.

7 Put the Calvados in a metal ladle or small saucepan, and gently heat until warm. Carefully set aflame with a match, let the flames die down, then stir into the sauce.

8 Serve the game hens with the sauce spooned on top and garnished with the caramelized apples and sprigs of fresh thyme.

DUCK WITH BERRY SAUCE

INGREDIENTS   Serves 4

4 boneless duck breasts,
  ½ lb. each
salt and freshly ground
  black pepper
1 tsp. corn oil

FOR THE SAUCE:
⅓ cup orange juice
1 bay leaf
3 tbsp. red currant jelly
¾ cup fresh or frozen
  mixed berries

2 tbsp. dried cranberries
  or cherries
½ tsp. light brown sugar
1 tbsp. balsamic vinegar
1 tsp. freshly chopped mint
sprigs of fresh mint, to garnish

TO SERVE:
freshly cooked potatoes
freshly cooked green beans

1 Remove the skins from the duck breasts and season with a little salt and pepper. Brush a griddle pan with the oil, then heat on the stove until smoking hot.

2 Place the duck skinned-side down in the pan. Cook over a medium-high heat for 5 minutes or until well browned. Turn the duck and cook for 2 minutes. Lower the heat and cook for an additional 5–8 minutes or until cooked, but still slightly pink in the center. Remove from the pan and keep warm.

3 While the duck is cooking, make the sauce. Put the orange juice, bay leaf, red currant jelly, fresh or frozen and dried berries, and sugar in a small griddle pan. Add any juices left in the griddle pan to the small pan. Slowly bring to a boil, lower the

heat, and simmer uncovered for 4–5 minutes or until the fruit is soft.

4 Remove the bay leaf. Stir in the vinegar and chopped mint, and season to taste with salt and pepper.

5 Slice the duck breasts diagonally, and arrange on serving plates. Spoon the berry sauce on top, and garnish with sprigs of fresh mint. Serve immediately with the potatoes and green beans.

HELPFUL HINT

Duck breasts are best served slightly pink in the center. Whole ducks, however, should be cooked thoroughly.

STICKY-GLAZED GAME HENS

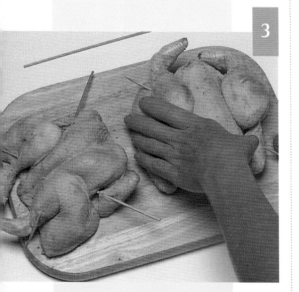

INGREDIENTS   Serves 4

2 game hens, each about
   1½ lbs.
salt and freshly ground
   black pepper
4 kumquats, thinly sliced
assorted lettuce leaves, crusty
   bread, and/or new potatoes,
   to serve

FOR THE GLAZE:
2 tbsp. finely grated
   lemon zest
1 tbsp. lemon juice
1 tbsp. dry sherry
2 tbsp. honey
2 tbsp. dark soy sauce
2 tbsp. mustard
1 tsp. tomato paste
½ tsp. Chinese five spice
   powder

1 Preheat the broiler just before cooking. Place one of the game hens breast-side down on a board. Using poultry shears, cut down one side of the backbone. Cut down the other side of the backbone. Remove the bone.

2 Open up the game hen and press down hard on the breastbone with the heel of your hand to break it and to flatten the game hen.

3 Thread 2 skewers crosswise through the bird to keep it flat, ensuring that each skewer goes through a wing and out through the leg on the opposite side. Repeat with the other bird. Season both sides of the bird with salt and pepper.

4 To make the glaze, mix together the lemon zest and juice, sherry, honey, soy sauce, mustard, tomato paste, and Chinese five spice powder, and use to brush over the game hens.

5 Place the game hens skin-side down on a broiler rack and broil under a medium heat for 15 minutes, brushing halfway through with more glaze.

6 Turn the game hens over and broil for 10 minutes. Brush again with glaze and arrange the kumquat slices on top. Broil for an additional 15 minutes until well browned and cooked through. If they brown too quickly, turn down the broiler.

7 Remove the skewers and cut each game hen in half along the breastbone. Serve immediately with the salad, crusty bread, and/or new potatoes.

THAI NOODLES & VEGETABLES WITH TOFU

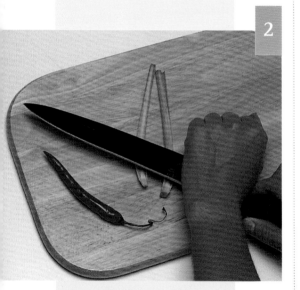

INGREDIENTS
Serves 4

¼ lb. firm tofu
2 tbsp. soy sauce
2 tsp. grated lime rind
2 lemongrass stalks
1 red chili
4 cups vegetable stock
2 slices fresh ginger, peeled
2 garlic cloves, peeled
2 sprigs of fresh cilantro
2½ cups dried egg noodles
1¾ cups shiitake or button
  mushrooms, sliced if large

2 carrots, peeled and cut into
  matchsticks
1 cup snow peas
2½ cups bok choy or other
  Chinese cabbage
1 tbsp. freshly chopped
  cilantro
salt and freshly ground
  black pepper
sprigs of fresh cilantro,
  to garnish

1 Drain the tofu well and cut into cubes. Put into a shallow dish with the soy sauce and lime rind. Stir well to coat, and leave to marinate for 30 minutes.

2 Meanwhile, put the lemongrass and chili on a chopping board and bruise with the side of a large knife, ensuring the blade is pointing away from your body. Put the vegetable stock in a large saucepan, and add the lemongrass, chili, ginger, garlic, and cilantro. Bring to a boil, cover, and simmer gently for 20 minutes.

3 Strain the stock into a clean saucepan. Return to a boil and add the noodles, tofu and its marinade, and the mushrooms. Simmer gently for 4 minutes.

4 Add the carrots, snow peas, bok choy, and cilantro, and simmer for an additional 3–4 minutes until the vegetables are just tender. Season to taste with salt and pepper. Garnish with cilantro sprigs and serve immediately.

FOOD FACT

Tofu is a curd derived from soybeans, and is an extremely protein-rich food that is virtually fat-free. Recent studies suggest that there are many health benefits to incorporating soy into your diet, not least of which are its cancer-prevention properties.

TAGLIATELLE WITH BROCCOLI & SESAME

INGREDIENTS   Serves 2

2⅔ cups broccoli, cut into florets

1 cup baby corn

1½ cups dried tagliatelle

1½ tbsp. tahini paste

1 tbsp. dark soy sauce

1 tbsp. dark brown sugar

1 tbsp. red wine vinegar

1 tbsp. corn oil

1 garlic clove, peeled and finely chopped

1-in. piece fresh ginger, peeled and shredded

½ tsp. dried chili flakes

salt and freshly ground black pepper

1 tbsp. toasted sesame seeds

slices of radish, to garnish

1 Bring a large saucepan of salted water to a boil, and add the broccoli and corn. Return the water to a boil, then using a slotted spoon, remove the vegetables at once, saving the water. Plunge them into cold water and drain well. Dry on paper towels and set aside.

2 Return the water to a boil. Add the tagliatelle and cook until al dente, or according to the package instructions. Drain well. Run under cold water, then drain well again.

3 Place the tahini, soy sauce, sugar, and vinegar into a bowl. Mix well, then set aside. Heat the oil in a wok or large skillet over a high heat and add the garlic, ginger, and chili flakes, and stir-fry for about 30 seconds. Add the broccoli and baby corn, and continue to stir-fry for about 3 minutes.

4 Add the tagliatelle to the wok along with the tahini mixture, and stir together for an additional 1–2 minutes until heated through. Season to taste with salt and pepper. Sprinkle with sesame seeds, garnish with the radish slices, and serve immediately.

FOOD FACT

Tahini is made from ground sesame seeds and is generally available in large supermarkets and Middle Eastern groceries. It is most often used in hummus.

PAD THAI NOODLES WITH MUSHROOMS

INGREDIENTS   Serves 4

2 cups flat rice noodles or rice
  vermicelli
1 tbsp. vegetable oil
2 garlic cloves, peeled and
  finely chopped
1 medium egg, lightly beaten
2 cups mixed mushrooms,
  such as shiitake, oyster, field,
  brown, and wild mushrooms
2 tbsp. lemon juice
1½ tbsp. Thai fish sauce

½ tsp. sugar
½ tsp. cayenne pepper
2 scallions, trimmed and cut
  into 1-in. pieces
¼ cup fresh bean sprouts

TO GARNISH:
chopped roasted peanuts
freshly chopped cilantro

1 Cook the noodles according to the package instructions. Drain well and set aside.

2 Heat a wok or large skillet. Add the oil and garlic. Cook until just golden. Add the egg and stir quickly to break it up.

3 Cook for a few seconds before adding the noodles and mushrooms. Scrape down the sides of the skillet to ensure they mix with the egg and garlic.

4 Add the lemon juice, fish sauce, sugar, cayenne pepper, scallions, and half of the bean sprouts, stirring quickly all the time.

5 Cook over a high heat for an additional 2–3 minutes until everything is heated through.

6 Turn onto a serving plate. Sprinkle with the remaining bean sprouts. Garnish with the chopped peanuts and cilantro, and serve immediately.

TASTY TIP

Far Eastern cooking is low-fat and often based around its fragrant spices. An aromatic alternative to this dish is to replace the lemon used in this dish with lemongrass. Discard the outer leaves, finely chop, and add with the other ingredients in Step 4.

PASTA WITH ZUCCHINI, ROSEMARY, & LEMON

INGREDIENTS   Serves 4

4½ cups dried pasta shapes,
  such as rigatoni
1½ tbsp. extra-virgin olive oil
2 garlic cloves, peeled and
  finely chopped
4 medium zucchini,
  thinly sliced
1 tbsp. freshly chopped
  rosemary
1 tbsp. freshly chopped parsley
2 tbsp. lemon zest

5 tbsp. lemon juice
2 tbsp. pitted ripe olives,
  coarsely chopped
2 tbsp. pitted green olives,
  coarsely chopped
salt and freshly ground
  black pepper

TO GARNISH:
lemon slices
sprigs of fresh rosemary

1 Bring a large saucepan of salted water to a boil and add the dried pasta.

2 Return to a boil and cook until al dente or according to the package instructions.

3 Meanwhile, when the pasta is almost done, heat the oil in a large skillet and add the garlic.

4 Cook over a medium heat until the garlic just begins to brown. Be careful not to overcook the garlic at this stage or it will become bitter.

5 Add the zucchini, rosemary, parsley, lemon zest, and juice. Cook for 3–4 minutes until the zucchini are just tender.

6 Add the olives to the skillet and stir well. Season to taste

with salt and pepper, and remove from the heat.

7 Drain the pasta well and add to the skillet. Stir until combined thoroughly. Garnish with lemon and sprigs of fresh rosemary, and serve immediately.

TASTY TIP

Look for pattypan squashes—small yellow or green squashes, shaped a little like flying saucers. They would make a good substitute for the zucchini in this recipe, as they have a similar flavor. Cut them in half vertically and cook as above.

VEGETARIAN SPAGHETTI BOLOGNESE

INGREDIENTS   Serves 4

2 tbsp. olive oil
1 onion, peeled and
  finely chopped
1 carrot, peeled and
  finely chopped
1 celery stick, trimmed and
  finely chopped
¼ lb. soy meat substitute, such
  as seitan

½ cup red wine
1¼ cups vegetable stock
1 tsp. ketchup
4 tbsp. tomato paste
4 cups dried spaghetti
4 tbsp. reduced-fat sour cream
salt and freshly ground
  black pepper
1 tbsp. freshly chopped parsley

1 Heat the oil in a large saucepan, and add the onion, carrot, and celery. Cook gently for 10 minutes, adding a little water if necessary, until softened and starting to brown.

2 Add the soy and cook an additional 2–3 minutes before adding the red wine. Increase the heat and simmer gently until nearly all the wine has evaporated.

3 Mix the vegetable stock and ketchup together, and add about half to the soy mixture, along with the tomato paste. Cover and simmer gently for about 45 minutes, adding the remaining stock as necessary.

4 Meanwhile, bring a large saucepan of salted water to a boil and add the spaghetti. Cook until al dente or according to the package instructions. Drain well.

Remove from the heat, add the sour cream, and season to taste with salt and pepper. Stir in the parsley, and serve immediately with the pasta.

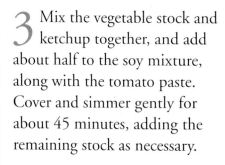

HELPFUL HINT

Quorn is a flavorful texturized vegetable protein high in fiber and low in fat. It is derived from the mushroom family and readily takes on any flavor it is cooked with. Use an equal portion of quorn and soy meat substitute for a change.

Spring Vegetable & Herb Risotto

INGREDIENTS   Serves 2–3

4 cups vegetable stock
½ cup asparagus
   tips, trimmed
1 cup baby carrots,
   scrubbed
½ cup peas, fresh
   or frozen
½ cup fine green
   beans, trimmed
1 tbsp. olive oil
1 onion, peeled and
   finely chopped

1 garlic clove, peeled and
   finely chopped
2 tsp. freshly chopped thyme
1 cup risotto rice
⅔ cup white wine
1 tbsp. each freshly chopped
   basil, chives, and parsley
1 tbsp. lemon zest
3 tbsp. reduced-fat sour cream
salt and freshly ground
   black pepper

1 Bring the vegetable stock to a boil in a large saucepan and add the asparagus, baby carrots, peas, and beans. Bring the stock back to a boil, and using a slotted spoon, remove the vegetables at once. Rinse under cold running water. Drain again and set aside. Keep the stock hot.

2 Heat the oil in a large, deep skillet and add the onion. Cook over a medium heat for 4–5 minutes until starting to brown. Add the garlic and thyme, and cook for a few seconds. Add the rice and stir well for a minute until the rice is hot and coated in oil.

3 Add the white wine and stir constantly until the wine is almost completely absorbed by the rice. Begin adding the stock, a ladleful at a time, stirring well and waiting until the last ladleful has been absorbed before stirring in the next. Add the vegetables after using about half of the stock. Continue until all the stock is used. This will take 20–25 minutes. The rice and vegetables should both be tender.

4 Remove the skillet from the heat. Stir in the herbs, lemon zest, and sour cream. Season to taste with salt and pepper, and serve immediately.

FOOD FACT

In Italy, they use different types of rice, such as Arborio and Carnaroli, depending on whether the risotto is vegetable- or meat-based.

BABY ONION RISOTTO

INGREDIENTS   Serves 4

FOR THE BABY ONIONS:
1 tbsp. olive oil
18 baby onions, peeled and
   halved if large
pinch of sugar
1 tbsp. freshly chopped thyme

FOR THE RISOTTO:
1 tbsp. olive oil
1 small onion, peeled
   and finely chopped
2 garlic cloves, peeled
   and finely chopped

1½ cups risotto rice
⅔ cup red wine
4 cups hot vegetable stock
½ cup reduced-fat goat cheese
salt and freshly ground
   black pepper
sprigs of fresh thyme,
   to garnish
arugula, to serve

1 For the baby onions, heat the olive oil in a saucepan and add the onions with the sugar. Cover and cook over a low heat, stirring occasionally, for 20–25 minutes until caramelized. Uncover during the last 10 minutes of cooking.

2 Meanwhile, for the risotto, heat the oil in a large skillet and add the onion. Cook over a medium heat for 5 minutes until softened. Add the garlic and cook for an additional 30 seconds.

3 Add the risotto rice and stir well. Add the red wine and stir constantly until the wine is almost completely absorbed by the rice. Begin adding the stock, a ladleful at a time, stirring well and waiting until the last ladleful has been absorbed before stirring in the next. It will take 20–25 minutes to add all the stock, by

which time the rice should be just cooked but still firm. Remove from the heat.

4 Add the thyme to the onions and cook briefly. Increase the heat and allow the onion mixture to boil for 2–3 minutes until almost evaporated. Add the onion mixture to the risotto along with the goat cheese. Stir well and season to taste with salt and pepper. Garnish with sprigs of fresh thyme. Serve immediately with the arugula.

FOOD FACT

To peel baby onions, put them into a saucepan of water and bring to a boil. Drain and run under cold water. The skins will loosen and peel easily.

VEGETABLE BIRYANI

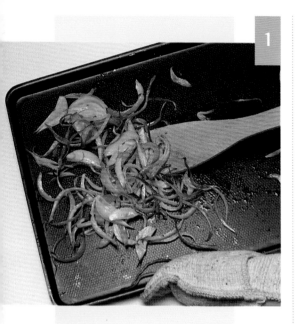

INGREDIENTS   Serves 4

2 tbsp. vegetable oil, plus a little extra for brushing

2 large onions, peeled and thinly sliced lengthwise

2 garlic cloves, peeled and finely chopped

1-in. piece fresh ginger, peeled and finely grated

1 small carrot, peeled and cut into sticks

1 small parsnip, peeled and diced

1 small sweet potato, peeled and diced

1 tbsp. medium curry paste

1 cup basmati rice

4 ripe tomatoes, peeled, seeded and diced

2½ cups vegetable stock

2 cups cauliflower florets

½ cup peas, defrosted if frozen

salt and freshly ground black pepper

TO GARNISH:

roasted cashews

raisins

fresh cilantro leaves

1 Preheat the oven to 400° F. Put 1 tablespoon of the vegetable oil in a large bowl with the onions and toss to coat. Lightly brush or spray a nonstick baking sheet with a little more oil. Spread half the onions on the baking sheet and cook on the top rack of the preheated oven for 25–30 minutes, stirring regularly until golden and crisp. Remove from the oven and set aside for the garnish.

2 Meanwhile, heat a large flameproof casserole dish over a medium heat, and add the remaining oil and onions. Cook for 5–7 minutes until softened and starting to brown. Add a little water if they start to stick. Add the garlic and ginger, and cook for another minute, then add the carrots, parsnips, and sweet potatoes. Cook the vegetables for an additional 5 minutes. Add the curry paste and stir for a minute until everything is coated, then stir in the rice and tomatoes. After 2 minutes, add the stock and stir well. Bring to a boil, cover, and simmer over a very gentle heat for about 10 minutes.

3 Add the cauliflower and peas, and cook for 8–10 minutes or until the rice is tender. Season to taste with salt and pepper. Serve garnished with the crispy onions, cashews, raisins, and cilantro.

TASTY TIP

Biryani is a dry dish. It is best served with a moist side dish.

BROWN RICE SPICED PILAF

INGREDIENTS

Serves 4

1 tbsp. vegetable oil
1 tbsp. blanched almonds, slivered or chopped
1 onion, peeled and chopped
1 carrot, peeled and diced
2 cups flat mushrooms, sliced thickly
¼ tsp. ground cinnamon
large pinch dried chili flakes
½ cup dried apricots, coarsely chopped
2 tbsp. currants
1 tbsp. orange zest
1½ cups brown basmati rice

3¾ cups vegetable stock
2 tbsp. freshly chopped cilantro
2 tbsp. freshly cut chives
salt and freshly ground black pepper
cut chives, to garnish

1 Preheat the oven to 400° F. Heat the oil in a large flameproof casserole dish and add the almonds. Cook for 1–2 minutes until just browning. Be very careful, as the nuts will burn easily.

2 Add the onion and carrot. Cook for 5 minutes until softened and starting to turn brown. Add the mushrooms and cook for an additional 5 minutes, stirring often.

3 Add the cinnamon and chili flakes, and cook for about 30 seconds before adding the apricots, currants, orange zest, and rice.

4 Stir together well and add the stock. Bring to a boil, cover tightly, and transfer to the preheated oven. Cook for 45 minutes until the rice and vegetables are tender.

5 Stir the cilantro and chives into the pilaf, and season to taste with salt and pepper. Garnish with the extra chives and serve immediately.

FOOD FACT

The less processed or refined the food, the higher the nutritional content. Brown basmati rice, in particular, is one of the best rices to eat, releasing carbohydrate slowly into the blood, thereby maintaining the body's energy levels, as well as supplying the body with fiber.

SPICED COUSCOUS & VEGETABLES

INGREDIENTS   Serves 4

1 tbsp. olive oil
1 large shallot, peeled and
   finely chopped
1 garlic clove, peeled and
   finely chopped
1 small red bell pepper,
   seeded and cut into strips
1 small yellow bell pepper,
   seeded and cut into strips
1 small eggplant, diced
1 tsp. each ground turmeric,
   cumin, ground cinnamon,
   and paprika
2 tsp. ground coriander

large pinch of saffron strands
2 tomatoes, peeled, seeded,
   and diced
2 tbsp. lemon juice
1¼ cups couscous
1 cup vegetable stock
2 tbsp. raisins
2 tbsp. whole almonds
2 tbsp. freshly chopped parsley
2 tbsp. freshly chopped
   cilantro
salt and freshly ground
   black pepper

1 Heat the oil in a large skillet, add the shallot and garlic, and cook for 2–3 minutes until softened. Add the bell peppers and eggplant, and reduce the heat.

2 Cook for 8–10 minutes until the vegetables are tender, adding a little water if necessary.

3 Test a piece of eggplant to ensure it is cooked through. Add all the spices and cook for an additional minute, stirring.

4 Increase the heat and add the tomatoes and lemon juice. Cook for 2–3 minutes until the tomatoes have started to break down. Remove from the heat and allow to cool slightly.

5 Meanwhile, put the couscous into a large bowl. Bring the

stock to a boil in a saucepan, then pour over the couscous. Stir well and cover with a clean dishtowel.

6 Allow to stand for 7–8 minutes until all the stock is absorbed and the couscous is tender.

7 Uncover the couscous and fluff with a fork. Stir in the vegetable and spice mixture along with the raisins, almonds, parsley, and cilantro. Season to taste with salt and pepper, and serve.

TASTY TIP

Although substantial enough to have as a main course, this dish would also be very nice served as a side dish.

BLACK BEAN CHILI WITH AVOCADO SALSA

INGREDIENTS   Serves 4

1½ cups black beans and black-eye peas, soaked overnight

2 tbsp. olive oil

1 large onion, peeled and finely chopped

1 red bell pepper, seeded and diced

2 garlic cloves, peeled and finely chopped

1 red chili, seeded and finely chopped

2 tsp. chili powder

1 tsp. ground cumin

2 tsp. ground coriander

14-oz. can tomatoes

2 cups vegetable stock

1 small ripe avocado, diced

½ small red onion, peeled and finely chopped

2 tbsp. freshly chopped cilantro

1 tbsp. lime juice

1 small tomato, peeled, seeded, and diced

salt and freshly ground black pepper

1 square unsweetened chocolate

TO GARNISH:

reduced-fat sour cream

lime slices

sprigs of cilantro

1 Drain the beans and place in a large saucepan with at least twice their volume of fresh water.

2 Bring slowly to a boil, skimming off any froth that rises to the surface. Boil rapidly for 10 minutes, then reduce the heat and simmer for about 45 minutes, adding more water if necessary. Drain and set aside.

3 Heat the oil in a large saucepan and add the onion and pepper. Cook for 3–4 minutes until softened. Add the garlic and chili. Cook for 5 minutes or until the onion and pepper have softened. Add the chili powder, cumin, and coriander, and cook for 30 seconds. Add the beans along with the tomatoes and stock.

4 Bring to a boil and simmer uncovered for 40–45 minutes until the beans and vegetables are tender and the sauce has reduced.

5 Mix together the avocado, onion, cilantro, lime juice, and tomato. Season with salt and pepper, and set aside. Remove the chili from the heat. Break the chocolate into pieces. Sprinkle over the chili. Let stand for 2 minutes. Stir well. Garnish with sour cream, lime, and cilantro. Serve with the avocado salsa.

BOSTON-STYLE BAKED BEANS

INGREDIENTS   Serves 8

2 cups mixed dried beans, such as kidney beans, lima beans, chickpeas, or pinto beans
1 large onion, peeled and finely chopped
5 tbsp. molasses
2 tbsp. mustard
2 tbsp. light brown sugar
1 cup all-purpose flour
1 cup fine cornmeal

2 tbsp. sugar
2½ tsp. baking powder
½ tsp. salt
2 tbsp. freshly chopped thyme
2 medium eggs
1 cup milk
2 tbsp. melted butter
salt and freshly ground black pepper
sprigs of fresh parsley, to garnish

1 Preheat the oven to 250° F. Put the beans into a large saucepan and cover with at least twice their volume of water. Bring to a boil, and simmer for 2 minutes. Allow to stand for 1 hour. Return to a boil, and boil rapidly for about 10 minutes. Drain and set aside.

2 Mix together the onion, molasses, mustard, and sugar in a large bowl. Add the drained beans and 1¼ cups fresh water. Stir well, bring to a boil, cover, and transfer to the preheated oven for 4 hours in an ovenproof dish, stirring once every hour and adding more water if necessary.

3 When the beans are cooked, remove from the oven and keep warm. Increase the oven temperature to 400° F. Mix together the all-purpose flour, cornmeal, sugar, baking powder, salt, and most of the thyme. Set aside about one third for the garnish. In a separate bowl, beat the eggs, then stir in the milk and butter. Pour the wet ingredients onto the dry ones and stir just enough to combine.

4 Pour into a buttered 7-inch square cake pan. Sprinkle with the remaining thyme. Cook for 30 minutes until golden and risen, or until a toothpick inserted into the center comes out clean. Cut into squares, then reheat the beans. Season to taste with salt and pepper, and serve immediately, garnished with parsley sprigs.

TASTY TIP

For those who are not vegetarians, add 1¼ cups cooked bacon to the beans as a tasty alternative.

PUMPKIN & CHICKPEA CURRY

INGREDIENTS   Serves 4

1 tbsp. vegetable oil
1 small onion, peeled
 and sliced
2 garlic cloves, peeled and
 finely chopped
1-in. piece ginger, peeled and
 grated
1 tsp. ground coriander
½ tsp. ground cumin
½ tsp. ground turmeric
¼ tsp. ground cinnamon
2 tomatoes, chopped
2 red bird's eye chilies, seeded
 and finely chopped

2½ cups pumpkin or butternut
 squash flesh, cubed
1 tbsp. hot curry paste
1¼ cups vegetable stock
1 large, firm banana
14-oz. can chickpeas, drained
 and rinsed
salt and freshly ground
 black pepper
1 tbsp. freshly chopped
 cilantro
sprigs of fresh cilantro,
 to garnish
rice or naan bread, to serve

1 Heat 1 tablespoon of the oil in a saucepan and add the onion. Cook gently for 5 minutes until softened.

2 Add the garlic, ginger, and spices, and cook for an additional minute. Add the chopped tomatoes and chilies, and cook for another minute.

3 Add the pumpkin and curry paste and cook for 3–4 minutes before adding the stock.

4 Stir well, bring to a boil, and simmer for 20 minutes until the pumpkin is tender.

5 Thickly slice the banana and add to the pumpkin along with the chickpeas. Simmer for an additional 5 minutes.

6 Season to taste with salt and pepper, and add the chopped cilantro. Serve immediately, garnished with cilantro sprigs and some rice or naan bread.

HELPFUL HINT

Curry pastes come in mild, medium, and hot varieties. Although hot curry paste is recommended in this recipe, use whichever one you prefer.

ROASTED MIXED VEGETABLES WITH GARLIC & HERB SAUCE

INGREDIENTS

Serves 4

1 large garlic bulb
1 large onion, peeled and cut
  into wedges
4 small carrots, peeled and
  quartered
4 small parsnips, peeled
6 small potatoes, scrubbed
  and halved
1 fennel bulb, sliced thickly
4 sprigs of fresh rosemary

4 sprigs of fresh thyme
2 tbsp. olive oil
salt and freshly ground
  black pepper
1 cup low-fat cream cheese
  with herbs and garlic
4 tbsp. milk
1 tbsp. lemon zest
sprigs of thyme, to garnish

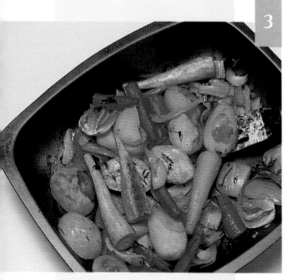

1 Preheat the oven to 425° F. Cut the garlic in half horizontally. Put into a large roasting pan with all the vegetables and herbs.

2 Add the oil, season well with salt and pepper, and toss together to coat lightly in the oil.

3 Cover with foil and roast in the preheated oven for 50 minutes. Remove the foil and cook for an additional 30 minutes until all the vegetables are tender and slightly charred.

4 Remove the pan from the oven and allow to cool.

5 In a small saucepan, melt the low-fat cream cheese together with the milk and lemon zest.

6 Remove the garlic from the roasting pan and squeeze the flesh into a bowl. Mash thoroughly, then add to the sauce. Heat through gently. Season the vegetables to taste. Pour some sauce into small ramekins and garnish with 4 sprigs of thyme. Serve immediately with the roasted vegetables and the sauce to dip.

TASTY TIP

This dish can also be served as a delicious accompaniment to any broiled or roasted fish, seafood, or chicken dish. Following the Mediterranean theme, marinate or drizzle the fish with a little olive oil, lemon juice, lemon rind, and mixed herbs.

ROASTED BUTTERNUT SQUASH

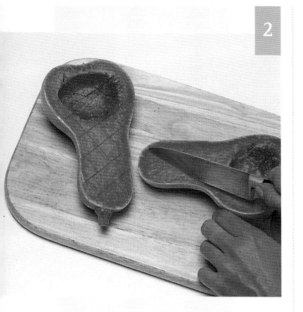

INGREDIENTS   Serves 4

2 small butternut squash
4 garlic cloves, peeled and
   crushed
1 tbsp. olive oil
salt and freshly ground
   black pepper
1 tbsp. oil
4 medium leeks, trimmed,
   cleaned, and thinly sliced
1 tbsp. black mustard seeds
11-oz. can lima beans, drained
   and rinsed

¾ cup fine green beans, halved
⅔ cup vegetable stock
1¼ cups arugula
2 tbsp. freshly cut chives

TO SERVE:
4 tbsp. reduced-fat sour cream
mixed salad

1 Preheat the oven to 400° F. Cut the butternut squash in half lengthwise and scoop out all of the seeds.

2 Cut the squash in a diamond pattern with a sharp knife. Mix the garlic with the olive oil, and brush over the cut surfaces of the squash. Season well with salt and pepper. Put on a baking sheet and roast for 40 minutes until tender.

3 Heat the oil in a saucepan and cook the leeks and mustard seeds for 5 minutes.

4 Add the drained lima beans, green beans, and vegetable stock. Bring to a boil, and simmer gently for 5 minutes until the green beans are tender.

5 Remove from the heat and stir in the arugula and chives.

Season well. Remove the squash from the oven and allow to cool for 5 minutes. Spoon in the bean mixture. Garnish with a few cut chives and serve immediately with the sour cream and a mixed salad.

HELPFUL HINT

If preferred, use dried lima beans instead of the canned variety. To cook dried beans, soak ⅔ cup dried lima beans in plenty of water overnight. Drain and put into a saucepan with at least twice their volume of fresh water. Bring to a boil and boil rapidly for 10 minutes, reduce the heat, and simmer gently for an additional 45–50 minutes until tender. Drain and use as above.

VEGETABLE CASSOULET

INGREDIENTS   Serves 6

⅔ cup dried kidney beans, soaked overnight

2 tbsp. olive oil

2 garlic cloves, peeled and chopped

9 baby onions, peeled and halved

2 carrots, peeled and diced

2 celery stalks, trimmed and finely chopped

1 red bell pepper, seeded and chopped

1½ cups mixed mushrooms, sliced

1 tbsp. each freshly chopped rosemary, thyme, and sage

⅔ cup red wine

4 tbsp. tomato paste

1 tbsp. dark soy sauce

salt and freshly ground black pepper

½ cup fresh bread crumbs

1 tbsp. freshly chopped parsley

sprigs of basil, to garnish

1 Preheat the oven to 375° F. Drain the kidney beans and place in a saucepan with 1 quart of fresh water. Bring to a boil, and boil rapidly for 10 minutes. Reduce the heat and simmer gently for 45 minutes. Drain the beans, setting aside 1¼ cups of the liquid.

2 Heat 1 tablespoon of the oil in a flameproof casserole dish and add the garlic, onions, carrot, celery, and red bell pepper. Cook gently for 10–12 minutes until tender and starting to brown. Add more water if the vegetables start to stick. Add the mushrooms and cook for an additional 5 minutes until softened. Add the herbs and stir briefly.

3 Stir in the red wine and boil rapidly for about 5 minutes until reduced and syrupy. Stir in the beans and their liquid, the tomato paste, and soy sauce. Season to taste with salt and pepper.

4 Mix together the bread crumbs and parsley with the remaining 1 tablespoon of oil. Sprinkle this mixture evenly over the top of the stew. Cover loosely with foil and transfer to the preheated oven. Cook for 30 minutes. Carefully remove the foil and cook for an additional 15–20 minutes until the topping is crisp and golden. Garnish with basil sprigs and serve immediately.

HELPFUL HINT

If cooking dried kidney beans is too time consuming, then use canned beans instead.

CREAMY LENTILS

INGREDIENTS   Serves 4

1¼ cups lentils
1 tbsp. olive oil
1 garlic clove, peeled and
  finely chopped
1 tbsp. lemon zest
2 tbsp. lemon juice
1 tsp. mustard
1 tbsp. freshly chopped
  tarragon
3 tbsp. reduced-fat sour cream

salt and freshly ground
  black pepper
2 small tomatoes, seeded and
  chopped
5 tbsp. pitted ripe olives
1 tbsp. freshly chopped
  parsley

TO GARNISH:

sprigs of fresh tarragon
lemon wedges

1 Put the lentils in a saucepan with plenty of cold water, and bring to a boil.

2 Boil rapidly for 10 minutes, reduce the heat, and simmer gently for an additional 20 minutes until tender. Drain well.

3 Meanwhile, prepare the dressing. Heat the oil in a skillet over a medium heat.

4 Add the garlic and cook for about a minute until just beginning to brown. Add the lemon zest and juice.

5 Add the mustard and cook for an additional 30 seconds.

6 Add the tarragon and sour cream, and season to taste with salt and pepper.

7 Simmer and add the drained lentils, tomatoes, and olives.

8 Transfer to a serving dish and sprinkle the chopped parsley on top.

9 Garnish the lentils with the tarragon sprigs and the lemon wedges, and serve immediately.

FOOD FACT

Puy lentils are smaller and fatter than green lentils, and have a mottled coloring, ranging from gold to green. They keep their shape and firm texture when cooked. They may not always be French, however, as this type of lentil is also grown extensively in Canada.

PEPERONATA

INGREDIENTS   Serves 6

2 red bell peppers
2 yellow bell peppers
1 lb. waxy potatoes
1 large onion
2 tbsp. good-quality virgin
  olive oil
2¼ cups tomatoes, peeled,
  seeded, and chopped

2 small zucchini
5 tbsp. pitted ripe olives,
  quartered
small handful basil leaves
salt and freshly ground
  black pepper
crusty bread, to serve

1 Prepare the bell peppers by halving them lengthwise and removing the stems, seeds, and membranes.

2 Cut the peppers lengthwise into strips about ½ inch wide. Peel the potatoes and cut into rough dice, about 1–1¼ inch across. Cut the onion lengthwise into 8 wedges.

3 Heat the olive oil in a large saucepan over a medium heat.

4 Add the onion and cook for about 5 minutes or until starting to brown.

5 Add the bell peppers, potatoes, tomatoes, zucchini, ripe olives, and about 4 torn basil leaves. Season to taste with salt and pepper.

6 Stir the mixture, cover, and cook over a very low heat for about 40 minutes or until the vegetables are tender but still hold their shape. Garnish with

the remaining basil. Transfer to a serving bowl and serve immediately with chunks of crusty bread.

FOOD FACT

This dish is delicious served with Parmesan melba toasts. To make, simply remove the crusts from 4 slices of thin white bread. Lightly toast and allow to cool before splitting each piece in half by slicing horizontally. Cut diagonally into triangles, place under a hot broiler, and toast each side for a few minutes until golden and curling at the edges. Sprinkle with finely shredded Parmesan cheese, and melt under the broiler.

MUSHROOM STEW

INGREDIENTS   Serves 4

¼ cup dried porcini
  mushrooms
2 lbs. assorted fresh
  mushrooms, wiped
2 tbsp. good-quality virgin
  olive oil
1 onion, peeled and finely
  chopped
2 garlic cloves, peeled and
  finely chopped
1 tbsp. fresh thyme leaves

pinch of ground cloves
salt and freshly ground
  black pepper
2¼ cups tomatoes, peeled,
  seeded, and chopped
2 cups instant polenta
2½ cups vegetable stock
3 tbsp. freshly chopped
  mixed herbs
sprigs of parsley, to garnish

1 Soak the porcini mushrooms in a small bowl of hot water for 20 minutes.

2 Drain and set aside the porcini mushrooms and their soaking liquid. Cut the fresh mushrooms in half and set aside.

3 In a saucepan, heat the oil and add the onion.

4 Cook gently for 5–7 minutes until softened. Add the garlic, thyme, and cloves, and continue cooking for 2 minutes.

5 Add all the mushrooms and cook for 8–10 minutes until the mushrooms have softened, stirring often. Season to taste with salt and pepper, and add the tomatoes and the soaking liquid.

6 Simmer, partly covered, over a low heat for about 20 minutes until thickened. Adjust the seasoning to taste.

7 Meanwhile, cook the polenta according to the package instructions using the vegetable stock. Stir in the herbs and divide among 4 dishes.

8 Spoon the mushrooms over the polenta, garnish with the parsley, and serve immediately.

TASTY TIP

For a dinner party version of this recipe, add a generous splash of red wine with the soaking liquid in step 5, and just before serving, remove from the heat and stir in 2 tablespoons of low-fat plain yogurt.

Huevos Rancheros

INGREDIENTS   Serves 4

2 tbsp. olive oil
1 large onion, peeled and
  finely chopped
1 red bell pepper, seeded and
  finely chopped
2 garlic cloves, peeled and
  finely chopped
2–4 green chilies, seeded and
  finely chopped
1 tsp. ground cumin
1 tsp. chili powder
2 tsp. ground coriander
2 tbsp. freshly chopped
  cilantro

2¼ cups ripe plum tomatoes,
  peeled, seeded, and coarsely
  chopped
¼ tsp. sugar
8 small eggs
4–8 flour tortillas
salt and freshly ground
  black pepper
sprigs of fresh cilantro,
  to garnish
refried beans, to
  serve (optional)

1 Heat the oil in a large, heavy saucepan. Add the onion and bell pepper, and cook over a medium heat for 10 minutes.

2 Add the garlic, chilies, ground cumin, chili powder, and chopped cilantro, and cook for an additional minute.

3 Add the tomatoes and sugar. Stir well, cover, and cook for 20 minutes. Uncover and cook for an additional 20 minutes.

4 Lightly poach the eggs in a large skillet filled with gently simmering water. Drain well and keep warm.

5 Place the tortillas briefly under a hot broiler. Turn once, then remove from the broiler when crisp.

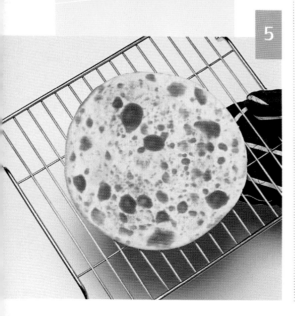

6 Add the freshly chopped cilantro to the tomato sauce and season to taste with salt and pepper.

7 To serve, arrange 2 tortillas on each serving plate, then place 2 eggs on the top and spoon the sauce over. Garnish with sprigs of fresh cilantro, and serve immediately with warm refried beans, if desired.

HELPFUL HINT

Although eggs are rich in protein, they also contain high levels of cholesterol and fat, so it is best to eat no more than 2–4 eggs per week.

EGGPLANT & YOGURT DIP

INGREDIENTS
Makes 2 cups

2 eggplants
1 tbsp. light olive oil
1 tbsp. lemon juice
2 garlic cloves, peeled and
  crushed
9-oz. jar pimientos, drained
⅔ cup low-fat plain yogurt

salt and freshly ground
  black pepper
2 tbsp. pitted ripe olives,
  chopped
1½ cups cauliflower florets
2⅔ cups broccoli florets
½ cup carrots, peeled and cut
  into 2-in. strips

1 Preheat the oven to 400° F. Pierce the skin of the eggplants with a fork and place on a baking sheet. Cook in the preheated oven for 40 minutes or until very soft.

2 Cool the eggplants, then cut in half and scoop out the flesh and tip into a bowl.

3 Mash the eggplant with the olive oil, lemon juice, and garlic for a few seconds in a food processor until blended.

4 Dice the pimientos and add to the eggplant mixture.

5 When blended, add the yogurt. Stir well and season to taste with salt and pepper.

6 Add the chopped olives and leave in the refrigerator to chill for at least 30 minutes.

7 Place the cauliflower and broccoli florets and carrot strips into a saucepan, and cover with boiling water. Simmer for 2 minutes, then rinse in cold water. Drain and serve as hors d'oeuvres to accompany the dip.

TASTY TIP

Following the Middle Eastern style of this dish, why not also serve pieces of warmed, unleavened bread such as naan or pita with this dip? To warm the bread, preheat the oven to 400° F, wrap in preheated foil, and place in the oven for 5–7 minutes, depending on the size of the bread.

BULGUR SALAD WITH MINTY LEMON DRESSING

INGREDIENTS

Serves 4

⅔ cup bulgur
4-in. piece cucumber
2 shallots, peeled
1 cup baby corn
3 ripe but firm tomatoes

FOR THE DRESSING:
1 tbsp. lemon rind
3 tbsp. lemon juice

3 tbsp. freshly chopped mint
2 tbsp. freshly chopped parsley
1–2 tsp. honey
2 tbsp. corn oil
salt and freshly ground
  black pepper

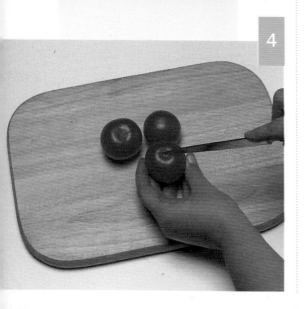

1 Place the bulgur in a large saucepan and cover with boiling water.

2 Simmer for about 10 minutes, then drain thoroughly and turn into a serving bowl.

3 Cut the cucumber into small dice, chop the shallots finely, and set aside. Steam the corn over a saucepan of boiling water for 10 minutes or until tender. Drain and slice into thick chunks.

4 Cut a cross on the top of each tomato, and place in boiling water until their skins start to peel away.

5 Remove the skins and the seeds, and cut the tomatoes into small dice.

6 Make the dressing by briskly whisking all the ingredients in a small bowl until mixed well.

7 When the bulgur has cooled a little, add all the prepared vegetables and stir in the dressing. Season to taste with salt and pepper, and serve.

FOOD FACT

This dish is loosely based on the Middle Eastern dish tabbouleh, a type of salad in which all the ingredients are mixed together and served cold.

CARROT & PARSNIP TERRINE

INGREDIENTS   Serves 8–10

3¾ cups carrots, peeled and
  chopped
2 cups parsnips, peeled and
  chopped
6 tbsp. reduced-fat sour cream
10 cups spinach, rinsed
1 tbsp. brown sugar
1 tbsp. freshly chopped parsley
½ tsp. freshly grated nutmeg
salt and freshly ground
  black pepper

6 medium eggs
sprigs of fresh basil,
  to garnish

FOR THE TOMATO COULIS:
1½ cups ripe tomatoes, seeded
  and chopped
1 medium onion, peeled and
  finely chopped

1 Preheat the oven to 400° F. Grease and line a 3 x 9 inch loaf pan with nonstick baking parchment. Cook the carrots and parsnips in boiling, salted water for 10–15 minutes or until very tender. Drain and purée separately. Add 2 tablespoons of sour cream to both the carrots and the parsnips.

2 Steam the spinach for 5–10 minutes or until very tender. Drain and squeeze out as much liquid as possible, then stir in the remaining sour cream.

3 Add the brown sugar to the carrot purée, the parsley to the parsnip mixture, and the nutmeg to the spinach. Season all to taste with salt and pepper.

4 Beat 2 eggs, add to the spinach, and turn into the prepared pan. Add another 2 beaten eggs to the carrot mixture

and layer carefully on top of the spinach. Beat the remaining eggs into the parsnip purée and layer on top of the terrine.

5 Place the pan in a baking dish and pour in enough hot water to come halfway up the sides of the pan. Cook for 1 hour until a toothpick inserted into the center comes out clean.

6 Let the terrine cool for at least 30 minutes. Run a sharp knife around the edges. Turn out onto a dish and set aside.

7 Make the tomato coulis by simmering the tomatoes and onions together for 5–10 minutes until thickened slightly.

8 Season to taste. Blend well in a blender or food processor and serve as an accompaniment to the terrine. Garnish with sprigs of basil and serve.

Chinese Salad with Soy & Ginger Dressing

INGREDIENTS   Serves 4

1 head of Chinese cabbage
7-oz. can water chestnuts,
 drained
6 scallions, trimmed
4 ripe but firm cherry
 tomatoes
1 cup snow peas
¾ cup bean sprouts
2 tbsp. freshly chopped
 cilantro

FOR THE DRESSING:
2 tbsp. corn oil
4 tbsp. light soy sauce
1-in. piece ginger, peeled and
 grated
2 tbsp. lemon zest
1 tbsp. lemon juice
salt and freshly ground
 black pepper
crusty white bread, to serve

1 Rinse and finely shred the Chinese cabbage and place in a serving dish.

2 Slice the water chestnuts into small slivers and cut the scallions diagonally into 1-inch lengths, then split lengthwise into thin strips.

3 Cut the tomatoes in half, then slice each half into 3 wedges, and set aside.

4 Simmer the snow peas in boiling water for 2 minutes until beginning to soften, drain, and cut in half diagonally.

5 Arrange the water chestnuts, scallions, snow peas, tomatoes, and bean sprouts on top of the shredded Chinese cabbage. Garnish with the freshly chopped cilantro.

6 Make the dressing by whisking all the ingredients together in a small bowl until mixed thoroughly. Serve with the bread and the salad.

TASTY TIP

A delicious alternative is to add some chicken. Cut 2 skinless chicken breasts into strips, place in a dish, and add 1 finely chopped clove of garlic, 2 tablespoons of light soy sauce, and 1 tablespoon of oil. Leave for 30 minutes, then cook in a hot skillet or wok for 5–10 minutes, stirring frequently. Serve on top of the salad with a sprinkling of sesame seeds.

CURLY ENDIVE & SEAFOOD SALAD

INGREDIENTS   Serves 4

1 head of curly endive
2 green bell peppers
5-in. piece cucumber
1 cup squid, cleaned and cut
    into thin rings
2 cups baby asparagus spears
4 thin smoked salmon slices,
    cut into wide strips
2 cups fresh cooked mussels,
    in their shells

FOR THE LEMON DRESSING:
2 tbsp. corn oil
1 tbsp. white wine vinegar
5 tbsp. fresh lemon juice
1–2 tsp. sugar
1 tsp. mild mustard
salt and freshly ground
    black pepper

TO GARNISH:
slices of lemon
sprigs of fresh cilantro

1 Rinse and tear the endive into small pieces and arrange on a serving platter.

2 Remove the seeds from the bell peppers and dice the peppers and cucumber. Sprinkle over the endive.

3 Bring a saucepan of water to a boil and add the squid rings. Bring the saucepan up to a boil again, then turn off the heat and let stand for 5 minutes. Drain and rinse thoroughly in cold water.

4 Cook the asparagus in boiling water for 5 minutes or until tender but just crisp. Arrange with the squid, smoked salmon, and mussels on top of the salad.

5 To make the lemon dressing, put all the ingredients into a screw-topped jar or into a small bowl, and mix thoroughly until the ingredients are combined.

6 Spoon 3 tablespoons of the dressing over the salad and serve the remainder in a small jug. Garnish the salad with slices of lemon and sprigs of cilantro, and serve.

TASTY TIP

Why not substitute a 1¼ cups diced cooked turkey breast for the seafood? Add 10 cooked baby new potatoes to the salad. Peel and halve 12 hard-boiled eggs, and use as a garnish. Pour the lemon dressing over the salad and serve.

WARM FRUITY RICE SALAD

INGREDIENTS

Serves 4

¾ cup mixed basmati and wild rice
¼ lb. skinless chicken breast
1¼ cups chicken or vegetable stock
¾ cup dried apricots
½ cup dried dates
3 celery stalks

FOR THE DRESSING:
2 tbsp. corn oil
1 tbsp. white wine vinegar
4 tbsp. lemon juice
1–2 tsp. honey, warmed
1 tsp. mustard
freshly ground black pepper

TO GARNISH:
6 scallions
sprigs of fresh cilantro

1 Place the rice in a saucepan of boiling, salted water and cook for 15–20 minutes or until tender. Rinse thoroughly with boiling water and set aside.

2 Meanwhile, wipe the chicken and place in a shallow saucepan with the stock.

3 Bring to a boil, cover, and simmer for about 15 minutes or until the chicken is cooked thoroughly and the juices run clear.

4 Leave the chicken in the stock until cool enough to handle, then cut into thin slices.

5 Chop the apricots and dates into small pieces. Peel any tough membranes from the outside of the celery and dice. Fold the apricots, dates, celery, and sliced chicken into the warm rice.

6 Make the dressing by whisking all the ingredients together in a small bowl until mixed thoroughly. Pour 2–3 tablespoons over the rice and stir in gently and evenly. Serve the remaining dressing separately.

7 Trim and chop the scallions. Sprinkle the scallions over the top of the salad, and garnish with the sprigs of cilantro. Serve while still warm.

HELPFUL HINT

It is very important that the chicken is cooked properly in Step 3. Some chicken breasts can be denser than others, so the best way to test is to cut into the thickest part of the meat and check that there is no pinkness.

HOT & SPICY RED CABBAGE WITH APPLES

INGREDIENTS

Serves 8

7 cups red cabbage, cored and shredded

2½ cups onions, peeled and finely sliced

2¾ cups apples, peeled, cored and finely sliced

½ tsp. mixed spices

1 tsp. ground cinnamon

2 tbsp. golden brown sugar

salt and freshly ground black pepper

2 tbsp. grated orange rind

1 tbsp. fresh orange juice

¼ cup medium-sweet apple cider (or apple juice)

2 tbsp. wine vinegar

TO SERVE:

reduced-fat sour cream

freshly ground black pepper

1 Preheat the oven to 300° F. Put just enough cabbage in a large casserole dish to cover the base evenly.

2 Place a layer of the onions and apples on top of the cabbage.

3 Sprinkle a little of the mixed spice, cinnamon, and sugar over the top. Season with salt and pepper.

4 Spoon over a small portion of the orange rind, orange juice, and the cider.

5 Continue to layer the casserole dish with the ingredients in the same order until used up.

6 Pour the vinegar as evenly as possible over the top layer of the ingredients.

7 Cover the casserole dish with a close-fitting lid, and cook in the preheated oven, stirring occasionally, for 2 hours until the cabbage is moist and tender. Serve immediately with the sour cream and black pepper.

TASTY TIP

This recipe uses wine vinegar, but this can be substituted with balsamic vinegar, which has a soft, sweet and sour, slightly fuller taste, and which will work well with the spices in this recipe. Balsamic vinegar is widely available and can be purchased in most supermarkets.

MARINATED VEGETABLE KABOBS

INGREDIENTS   Serves 4

2 small zucchini, cut into
   ¾-in. pieces
½ green bell pepper, seeded
   and cut into 1-in. pieces
½ red bell pepper, seeded and
   cut into 1-in. pieces
½ yellow bell pepper, seeded
   and cut into 1-in. pieces
8 baby onions, peeled
8 button mushrooms
8 cherry tomatoes

freshly chopped parsley,
   to garnish
couscous, to serve

FOR THE MARINADE:
1 tbsp. light olive oil
4 tbsp. dry sherry
2 tbsp. light soy sauce
1 red chili, seeded and finely
   chopped
2 garlic cloves, peeled and
   crushed
1-in. piece ginger, peeled and
   finely grated

1 Place the zucchini, bell peppers, and baby onions in a saucepan of just-boiled water. Bring back to a boil, and simmer for about 30 seconds.

2 Drain and rinse the cooked vegetables in cold water, and dry on absorbent paper towels.

3 Thread the cooked vegetables, mushrooms, and tomatoes alternately onto skewers and place in a large, shallow dish.

4 Make the marinade by beating all the ingredients together until blended thoroughly. Pour the marinade evenly over the kabobs, then chill in the refrigerator for at least 1 hour. Spoon the marinade over the kabobs occasionally during this time.

5 Place the kabobs in a hot griddle pan or on a hot barbecue, and cook gently for 10–12 minutes. Turn the kabobs frequently, and brush with the marinade when needed. When the vegetables are tender, sprinkle with chopped parsley, and serve immediately with couscous.

TASTY TIP

If using wooden skewers and cooking over a barbecue, soak in cold water for 30 minutes before using. Although these kabobs use only vegetables, large chunks of fish, such as cod or jumbo shrimp, could be added alternately between the vegetables and cooked as in Step 5.

PUMPKIN PÂTÉ

INGREDIENTS   Serves 8–10

1 lb. fresh pumpkin flesh
   (when in season), peeled, or
   15-oz. can pumpkin purée
1 tsp. corn oil
1 small onion, peeled and
   finely chopped
½ orange bell pepper, seeded
   and finely chopped
2 medium eggs, beaten
3 tbsp. low-fat plain yogurt
1 cup reduced-fat hard cheese,
   such as cheddar, shredded
¼ cup wheat germ

1 tbsp. freshly chopped
   oregano
salt and freshly ground
   black pepper
fresh salad leaves and crusty
   bread, to serve

1 Preheat the oven to 350° F. Grease and line a 3 x 9 inch loaf pan. Cut the pumpkin into cubes, and place in a saucepan of boiling water.

2 Simmer for 20 minutes or until the pumpkin is very tender. Drain and allow to cool, then mash well to form a purée.

3 Heat the oil in a nonstick skillet, and cook the chopped onion and pepper for about 4 minutes until softened.

4 Mix together the puréed pumpkin, softened vegetables, eggs, and yogurt. Add the cheese, wheat germ, and oregano. Season with salt and pepper.

5 When the pumpkin mixture is well blended, spoon it into the prepared pan and stand in a baking dish. Fill the tray with hot water to come halfway up the sides of the pan, and carefully place in the preheated oven.

6 Cook for about 1 hour or until firm, then leave to cool. Chill in the refrigerator for 30 minutes before turning out onto a serving plate. Serve with crusty bread and a fresh salad.

TASTY TIP

This pâté, after being mixed together in Step 4, could also be used to stuff fresh pasta. Serve the pasta tossed in a little extra-virgin olive oil and some coarsely torn, fresh sage leaves.

SPANISH BAKED TOMATOES

INGREDIENTS   Serves 4

¾ cup brown rice
2½ cups vegetable stock
2 tsp. corn oil
2 shallots, peeled and finely chopped
1 garlic clove, peeled and crushed
1 green bell pepper, seeded and diced
1 red chili, seeded and finely chopped
½ cup button mushrooms, finely chopped

1 tbsp. freshly chopped oregano
salt and freshly ground black pepper
4 large ripe tomatoes
1 large egg, beaten
1 tsp. sugar
basil leaves, to garnish
crusty bread, to serve

1 Preheat the oven to 350° F. Place the rice in a saucepan, pour in the vegetable stock, and bring to a boil. Simmer gently for 30 minutes or until the rice is tender. Drain and turn into a large bowl.

2 Add 1 teaspoon of corn oil to a small nonstick skillet and cook the shallots, garlic, bell pepper, chili, and mushrooms for 2 minutes. Add to the rice, along with the chopped oregano. Season with salt and pepper.

3 Slice the top off each tomato. Cut and scoop out the flesh, removing the hard core. Pass the tomato flesh through a strainer. Add 1 tablespoon of the juice to the rice mixture. Stir in the beaten egg, and mix. Sprinkle sugar in the base of each tomato. Pile the rice mixture into the shells.

4 Place the tomatoes in a baking dish and pour a little cold water around them. Replace their lids and drizzle a few drops of corn oil over the tops.

5 Cook in the preheated oven for about 25 minutes. Garnish with the basil leaves and season with black pepper. Serve immediately with crusty bread.

TASTY TIP

This dish is also delicious when made with meat. Add ¼ lb. of lean ground beef in Step 2. Heat the skillet and fry the meat on a high heat until cooked through and brown, before adding the rest of the ingredients.

STUFFED ONIONS WITH PINE NUTS

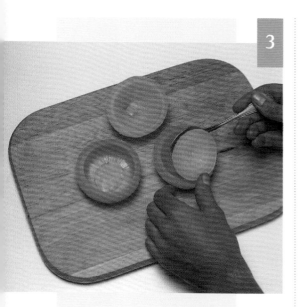

INGREDIENTS

Serves 4

4 medium onions, peeled
2 garlic cloves, peeled and crushed
2 tbsp. fresh whole-wheat bread crumbs
2 tbsp. fresh white bread crumbs
2 tbsp. golden raisins
4 tbsp. pine nuts

½ cup reduced-fat hard cheese, such as cheddar, shredded, plus extra for sprinkling
2 tbsp. freshly chopped parsley
1 medium egg, beaten
salt and freshly ground black pepper
lettuce leaves, to serve

1 Preheat the oven to 400° F. Bring a saucepan of water to a boil, then add the onions and cook gently for about 15 minutes.

2 Drain well. Let the onions cool, then slice each one in half horizontally.

3 Scoop out most of the onion flesh, but leave a reasonably firm shell.

4 Chop up 4 tablespoons of the onion flesh and place in a bowl with the garlic, bread crumbs, golden raisins, pine nuts, shredded cheese, and parsley.

5 Mix the bread-crumb mixture together thoroughly. Bind together with as much of the beaten egg as necessary to make a firm filling. Season to taste with salt and pepper.

6 Pile the mixture back into the onion shells, and sprinkle with some shredded cheese. Place on a greased baking sheet and cook in the preheated oven for 20–30 minutes or until golden brown. Serve immediately with the lettuce leaves.

FOOD FACT

While this dish is delicious on its own, it also complements barbecued meat and fish. The onion takes on a mellow, nutty flavor when cooked.

WARM LEEK & TOMATO SALAD

INGREDIENTS   Serves 4

1 lb. baby leeks, trimmed
2 medium ripe tomatoes
2 shallots, peeled and cut into
   thin wedges

1 tbsp. light olive oil
1 tsp. mustard
salt and freshly ground
   black pepper

FOR THE DRESSING:
2 tbsp. honey
2 tsp. grated lime rind
4 tbsp. lime juice

TO GARNISH:
freshly chopped tarragon
freshly chopped basil

1 Trim the leeks so that they are all the same length. Place in a steamer over a saucepan of boiling water, and steam for 8 minutes or until just tender.

2 Drain the leeks thoroughly and arrange in a shallow serving dish.

3 Make a cross in the top of the tomatoes, place in a bowl, and cover them with boiling water until their skins start to peel away. Remove from the bowl and carefully remove the skins.

4 Quarter the tomatoes, remove the seeds, then dice. Spoon over the top of the leeks, along with the shallots.

5 In a small bowl, make the dressing by whisking the honey, lime rind, lime juice, olive oil, mustard, salt, and pepper. Pour 3 tablespoons of the dressing over the leeks and tomatoes, and garnish with the tarragon and

basil. Serve while the leeks are still warm, with the remaining dressing served separately.

HELPFUL HINT

An easy way to measure honey is to plunge a metal measuring spoon into boiling water. Drain the spoon, then dip into the honey.

HELPFUL HINT

Really flavorful tomatoes can make all the difference to tomato dishes. Use plum or vittoria tomatoes, as they have been left on the vine longer to ripen, and therefore have a better flavor.

WINTER COLESLAW

INGREDIENTS   Serves 6

½ lb. white cabbage
1 medium red onion, peeled
½ lb. carrots, peeled
1 head celeriac, peeled
2 celery stalks, trimmed
½ cup golden raisins

FOR THE DRESSING:
⅔ cup low-fat plain yogurt
1 garlic clove, peeled and
  crushed
1 tbsp. lemon juice
1 tsp. honey
1 tbsp. freshly cut chives

1 Remove the hard core from the cabbage with a small knife and shred finely.

2 Slice the onion finely and coarsely grate the carrot.

3 Place the raw vegetables in a large bowl and mix together.

4 Cut the celeriac into thin strips and simmer in boiling water for about 2 minutes.

5 Drain the celeriac and rinse thoroughly with cold water.

6 Chop the celery, add to the bowl with the celeriac and golden raisins, and mix well.

7 Make the yogurt and herb dressing by briskly beating the yogurt, garlic, lemon juice, honey, and chives together.

8 Pour the dressing over the top of the salad. Stir the vegetables thoroughly to coat evenly, and serve.

TASTY TIP

To make cheese coleslaw, simply replace the golden raisins with 3 oz. of reduced-fat cheese. Whether the winter or cheese variety, coleslaw is particularly good with baked potatoes and a little low-fat spread.

HELPFUL HINT

This dish is delicious all year round, and can be served as an accompaniment to many dishes, including salads, baked potatoes, roulades, and fish.

MEDITERRANEAN FEAST

INGREDIENTS   Serves 4

1 small head of lettuce
1½ cups fine green beans
8 oz. baby new potatoes, scrubbed
4 medium eggs
1 green bell pepper
1 medium onion, peeled
7-oz. can tuna in water, drained and flaked into small pieces
½ cup reduced-fat hard cheese, such as cheddar, cut into small cubes
8 ripe but firm cherry tomatoes, quartered

5 tbsp. pitted ripe olives, halved
freshly chopped basil, to garnish

FOR THE LIME VINAIGRETTE:
3 tbsp. light olive oil
2 tbsp. white wine vinegar
4 tbsp. lime juice
2 tsp. grated lime rind
1 tsp. mustard
1-2 tsp. sugar
salt and freshly ground black pepper

1 Quarter the lettuce and remove the hard core. Tear into bite-size pieces and arrange on a large serving platter or four individual plates.

2 Cook the green beans in boiling, salted water for 8 minutes, and the potatoes for 10 minutes or until tender. Drain and rinse in cold water until cool, then cut both the beans and potatoes in half with a sharp knife.

3 Boil the eggs for 10 minutes, then rinse thoroughly under cold running water until cool. Remove the shells under the water, then cut each egg into 4.

4 Remove the seeds from the bell pepper and cut into thin strips. Finely chop the onion.

5 Arrange the beans, potatoes, eggs, bell peppers, and onion on top of the lettuce. Add the tuna, cheese, and tomatoes. Sprinkle with the olives and garnish with the basil.

6 To make the vinaigrette, place all the ingredients in a screw-top jar, and shake vigorously until everything is mixed thoroughly. Spoon 4 tablespoons over the top of the prepared salad, and serve the remainder separately.

FOOD FACT

Cans of tuna now include varieties such as albacore and yellowfin. Always choose tuna steaks over chunks.

BEET & POTATO MEDLEY

INGREDIENTS

Serves 4

¾ lb. raw baby beets
½ tsp. corn oil
8 oz. new potatoes
½ cucumber, peeled
3 tbsp. white wine vinegar
⅔ cup low-fat plain yogurt
salt and freshly ground
   black pepper

fresh lettuce leaves
1 tbsp. freshly cut chives,
   to garnish

1 Preheat the oven to 350° F. Scrub the beets thoroughly and place on a large baking sheet.

2 Brush the beets with a little oil and cook for 1½ hours or until a toothpick is easily inserted. Allow to cool slightly, then remove the skins from the beets.

3 Cook the potatoes in boiling water for about 10 minutes. Rinse in cold water and drain. Set the potatoes aside until cool. Dice evenly.

4 Cut the cucumber into cubes and place in a mixing bowl. Chop the beets into small cubes, and add to the bowl with the potatoes. Gently mix the vegetables together.

5 Mix together the vinegar and yogurt, and season to taste with a little salt and pepper. Pour over the vegetables and combine gently.

6 Arrange on a bed of lettuce leaves garnished with the cut chives, and serve.

HELPFUL HINT

Beets can also be cooked in the microwave. Place in a microwavable bowl. Add sufficient water to come halfway up the sides of the bowl. Cover and cook for 10–15 minutes on high. Leave for 5 minutes before removing the paper. Cool before peeling.

FOOD FACT

Like other fruits and vegetables that are red in color, beets have particularly high levels of antioxidants, which are essential to the body for fighting diseases.

LIGHT RATATOUILLE

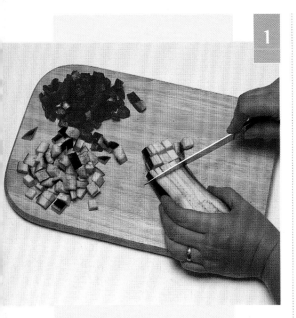

INGREDIENTS   Serves 4

1 red bell pepper
2 zucchini, trimmed
1 small eggplant, trimmed
1 onion, peeled
2 ripe tomatoes
1½ cups button mushrooms,
    wiped and halved or
    quartered

¾ cup tomato juice
1 tbsp. freshly chopped basil
salt and freshly ground
    black pepper

1 Seed the peppers, remove the membrane with a small sharp knife, and dice. Thickly slice the zucchini and dice the eggplant. Slice the onion into rings.

2 Place the tomatoes in boiling water until their skins begin to peel away.

3 Remove the skins from the tomatoes, cut into quarters, and remove the seeds.

4 Place all the vegetables in a saucepan with the tomato juice and basil. Season to taste with salt and pepper.

5 Bring to a boil, cover, and simmer for 15 minutes or until the vegetables are tender.

6 Remove the vegetables with a slotted spoon and arrange in a serving dish.

7 Bring the liquid in the saucepan to a boil and boil for 20 seconds or until it is slightly thickened. Season the sauce to taste with salt and pepper.

8 Pass the sauce through a strainer to remove some of the seeds, and pour over the vegetables. Serve the ratatouille hot or cold.

TASTY TIP

This dish would be perfect, served as an accompaniment to any of the fish dishes in this book. It is also delicious in an omelette or as a baked-potato filling.

SICILIAN BAKED EGGPLANT

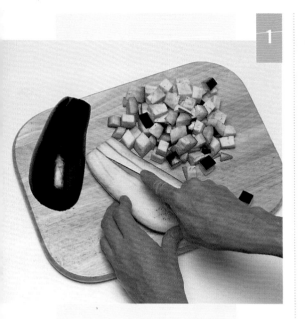

INGREDIENTS   Serves 4

1 large eggplant, trimmed
2 celery stalks, trimmed
4 large ripe tomatoes
1 tsp. corn oil
2 shallots, peeled and finely
  chopped
1½ tsp. tomato paste
2 tbsp. pitted green olives

2 tbsp. pitted ripe olives
salt and freshly ground
  black pepper
1 tbsp. white wine vinegar
2 tsp. sugar
1 tbsp. freshly chopped basil,
  to garnish
mixed lettuce leaves, to serve

1 Preheat the oven to 400° F. Cut the eggplant into small cubes and place on a greased baking sheet.

2 Cover the baking sheet with foil and cook in the preheated oven for about 15–20 minutes or until soft. Set aside to let the eggplant cool.

3 Place the celery and tomatoes in a large bowl, and cover with boiling water.

4 Remove the tomatoes from the bowl when their skins begin to peel away. Remove the skins, then seed and chop the flesh into small pieces.

5 Remove the celery from the bowl of water, finely chop, and set aside.

6 Pour the vegetable oil into a nonstick saucepan, add the chopped shallots, and cook gently for 2–3 minutes until soft. Add the celery, tomatoes, tomato

paste, and olives. Season to taste with salt and pepper.

7 Simmer gently for 3–4 minutes. Add the vinegar, sugar, and cooled eggplant to the saucepan and heat gently for 2–3 minutes until all the ingredients are well blended. Set aside to let the eggplant mixture cool. When cool, garnish with the chopped basil and serve with lettuce leaves.

FOOD FACT

It has been suggested that foods that are purple in color, such as eggplants, have particularly powerful antioxidants, which help the body protect itself from disease and strengthen the organs.

CARROT, CELERIAC, & SESAME SEED SALAD

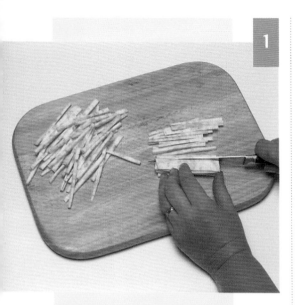

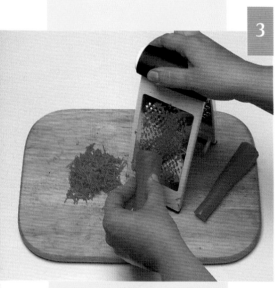

INGREDIENTS

Serves 6

1 head celeriac
2 medium carrots, peeled
5 tbsp. seedless raisins
2 tbsp. sesame seeds
freshly chopped parsley,
  to garnish

FOR THE DRESSING:
1 tbsp. grated lemon rind
4 tbsp. lemon juice
2 tbsp. corn oil
2 tbsp. honey
1 red bird's eye chili, seeded
  and finely chopped
salt and freshly ground
  black pepper

1 Slice the celeriac into thin matchsticks. Place in a small saucepan of boiling, salted water, and boil for 2 minutes.

2 Drain and rinse the celeriac in cold water, and place in a mixing bowl.

3 Finely grate the carrot. Add the carrot and the raisins to the celeriac in the bowl.

4 Place the sesame seeds under a hot broiler or fry in a skillet for 1–2 minutes or until golden brown, then allow to cool.

5 Make the dressing by beating together the lemon rind, lemon juice, oil, honey, chili, and seasoning, or by shaking thoroughly in a screw-top jar.

6 Pour 2 tablespoons of the dressing over the salad and toss well. Turn into a serving dish, and sprinkle over the toasted sesame seeds and chopped parsley. Serve the remaining dressing separately.

FOOD FACT

Celeriac is a root vegetable that is similar in taste to fennel, but with a texture closer to parsnips. This versatile vegetable has a creamy taste and is also delicious in soups and gratins.

CRISPY BAKED POTATOES WITH PROSCIUTTO

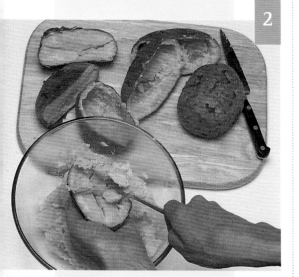

INGREDIENTS　　　　　　　　　　Serves 4

4 large baking potatoes
4 tsp. reduced-fat sour cream
salt and freshly ground
　black pepper
2 slices lean serrano ham or
　prosciutto, with fat removed
1 cup cooked baby fava beans
¼ cup cooked carrots, diced

1 cup cooked peas
½ cup reduced-fat hard cheese
　such as cheddar, shredded
fresh green salad, to serve

1 Preheat the oven to 400° F. Scrub the potatoes dry. Prick with a fork and place on a baking sheet. Cook for 1–1½ hours or until tender when squeezed. Use oven mitts to pick up the potatoes, as they will be very hot.

2 Cut the potatoes in half horizontally and scoop out all the flesh into a bowl.

3 Spoon the sour cream into the bowl and mix thoroughly with the potatoes. Season to taste with a little salt and pepper.

4 Cut the ham or prosciutto into fine strips, and carefully stir into the potato mixture with the fava beans, carrots, and peas.

5 Pile the mixture back into the 8 potato shells and sprinkle a little shredded cheese over the top.

6 Place under a hot broiler and cook until golden and heated through. Serve immediately with a fresh green salad.

FOOD FACT

Produced in Spain, serrano ham has a succulent, sweet taste and is traditionally carved along the grain. The nearest substitute is prosciutto. Serrano ham has a chewy texture and is often served in thin slices on bread.

ORANGE FREEZE

INGREDIENTS   Serves 4

4 large oranges
1¼ cups vanilla ice cream
2 cups raspberries

1½ cups confectioners' sugar,
plus extra for dusting
red currant sprigs, to decorate

1 Using a sharp knife, carefully cut the top off each orange.

2 Scoop out the flesh from the orange, discarding any seeds and thick pith.

3 Place the peels and tops in the freezer, and chop any remaining orange flesh.

4 Beat together the orange juice, orange flesh, and vanilla ice cream until well blended.

5 Cover and freeze for about 2 hours, occasionally breaking up the ice crystals with a fork. Stir the mixture from around the edge of the container into the center, then level and return to the freezer. Do this 2–3 times, then leave until it is almost frozen solid.

6 Place a large scoop of the ice-cream mixture into the frozen peels. Add another scoop on top, so that there is plenty outside of the orange shell, and return to the freezer for 1 hour.

7 Arrange the lids on top and freeze for an additional 2 hours until the filled orange peel is completely frozen solid.

8 Meanwhile, using a nylon strainer, press the raspberries into a bowl using the back of a wooden spoon, and mix together with the confectioners' sugar. Spoon the raspberry coulis onto four serving plates and place an orange at the center of each. Dust with confectioners' sugar and serve decorated with the red currants.

TASTY TIP

The fresh citrus in this dish works to clear the palate. The acidity combines well with the creaminess of the ice cream. Oranges are very good with mangoes, so why not experiment by adding the flesh of a small, ripe mango in step 4 for a more fragrant dessert? Lemons would also work well in this recipe.

CHOCOLATE MOUSSE

INGREDIENTS   Serves 6

6 squares milk or
   unsweetened chocolate
1 lb. can reduced-fat,
   crème anglaise
2 cups reduced-fat cream

12 physallis or cherries,
   to decorate
reduced-fat cookies, to serve

1 Break the chocolate into segments and place in a bowl set over a saucepan of simmering water. Leave until melted, stirring occasionally. Remove the bowl in the saucepan from the heat, and allow the melted chocolate to cool slightly.

2 Place the custard in a bowl, and using a metal spoon or rubber spatula, fold the melted chocolate into it. Stir well until completely combined.

3 Pour the cream into a small bowl and beat until the cream forms soft peaks.

4 Using a metal spoon or rubber spatula, fold in most of the whipped cream into the chocolate mixture.

5 Spoon into 6 tall glasses and carefully top with the remaining cream.

6 Leave the desserts to chill in the refrigerator for at least 1 hour or preferably overnight.

7 Decorate the chocolate desserts with a few cherries and serve with some reduced-fat cookies.

FOOD FACT

Cape gooseberries are also known as "physallis" and can be found in gourmet supermarkets. They have a sweet flavor with a slight acidity. They are similar in taste to passion fruit.

HELPFUL HINT

Have fun with the presentation of this dish. Why not serve in large cappuccino cups and lightly dust with some cocoa or confectioners' sugar. Serve plenty of cherries on the side, for guests to dip into the chocolate mousse.

CREAMY PUDDINGS WITH MIXED BERRY COMPOTE

INGREDIENTS

Serves 6

1 cup reduced-fat cream
9 oz. ricotta cheese
¼ cup sugar
4 squares white chocolate, broken into pieces

2 cups mixed summer fruits such as strawberries, blueberries, and raspberries
2 tbsp. Cointreau

1 Beat the cream until soft peaks form. Fold in the ricotta cheese and half the sugar.

2 Place the chocolate in a bowl set over a saucepan of simmering water. Stir until melted.

3 Remove from the heat and allow to cool, stirring occasionally. Stir into the cheese mixture until well blended.

4 Spoon the mixture into 6 individual pudding molds and level the surface of each pudding with the back of a spoon. Place in the freezer and freeze for 4 hours.

5 Place the fruits and remaining sugar in a saucepan and heat, stirring occasionally, until the sugar has dissolved and the juices are beginning to run. Stir in the Cointreau to taste.

6 Dip the pudding molds in hot water for 30 seconds and invert onto six serving plates. Spoon the fruit compote over the desserts and serve immediately.

TASTY TIP

Don't just save this recipe for the summer. Why not try mulled fruit compote with this recipe? Poach 4–6 dark plums, quartered, and 4 dessert pears, sliced into thick wedges, in ⅔ cup of red wine. Add 1 mulled wine sachet, 1–2 tablespoons of sugar, and 2 cinnamon sticks. Simmer until reduced by half and the plums and pears are softened. Remove from the heat and discard the mulled wine sachet. Allow to cool a little before spooning over the dessert. Decorate with fine strips of orange rind.

RICE PUDDING

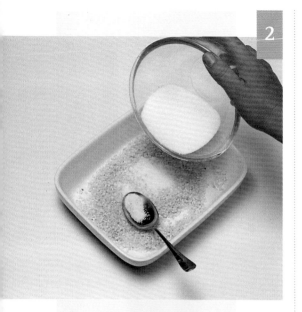

INGREDIENTS   Serves 4

¾ cup pudding rice
¼ cup granulated sugar
14-oz. can light evaporated
  milk
1¼ cups low-fat milk

pinch of freshly grated
  nutmeg
¼ stick reduced-fat butter
reduced-sugar jelly,
  to decorate

1 Preheat the oven to 300° F.
Lightly grease a large
ovenproof dish.

2 Sprinkle the rice and sugar
into the dish, and mix
together.

3 Bring the evaporated milk
and milk to a boil in a small
saucepan, stirring occasionally.

4 Stir the milks into the rice
and mix well until the rice is
coated thoroughly.

5 Sprinkle with the nutmeg,
cover with foil, and cook in
the preheated oven for 30 minutes.

6 Remove the pudding from
the oven and stir well,
breaking up any lumps.

7 Cover with the same foil and
cook for an additional 30
minutes. Remove from the oven
and stir well again.

8 Dot the pudding with butter
and cook for an additional
45–60 minutes until the rice is
tender and the skin is browned.

9 Divide the pudding among 4
individual serving bowls. Top
with a large spoonful of the jelly
and serve immediately.

TASTY TIP

Traditionally, rice pudding was
cooked alongside the Sunday
roast which, after many hours
in the oven, came out rich and
creamy. The main trick to
achieving traditional creamy
rice pudding is not using
cream and whole milk, but
instead long, slow cooking
on a low temperature. Try
adding a few golden raisins
and lemon peel, or a few
coarsely crushed cardamom
pods for an alternative flavor.
It is also delicious dusted with
a little ground cinnamon.

LEMON SURPRISE

INGREDIENTS
Serves 4

½ stick reduced-fat butter
¾ cup sugar
3 medium eggs, separated
¾ cup self-rising flour
2 cups low-fat milk
4 tbsp. lemon juice

3 tbsp. orange juice
2 tsp. confectioners' sugar
lemon twists, to decorate
sliced strawberries, to serve

1 Preheat the oven to 375° F. Lightly grease a deep ovenproof dish.

2 Beat together the butter and sugar until pale and fluffy.

3 Add the egg yolks, one at a time, with 1 tablespoon of the flour, and beat well after each addition. Once added, stir in the remaining flour.

4 Stir in the milk, the lemon juice, and the orange juice.

5 Beat the egg whites until stiff, and fold into the dessert mixture with a metal spoon or rubber spatula until well combined. Pour into the prepared dish.

6 Stand the dish in a roasting pan and pour in just enough boiling water to come halfway up the sides of the dish.

7 Cook in the preheated oven for 45 minutes until well risen and spongy to the touch.

8 Remove the dessert from the oven and sprinkle with the confectioners' sugar. Decorate with the lemon twists and serve immediately with the strawberries.

FOOD FACT

This recipe uses a bain-marie, (when the dish is placed in a pan as in Step 6), which enables the pudding to cook slower. This is necessary, as reduced-fat butter does not respond well when cooked at higher temperatures.

ORANGE CURD & PLUM PUDDINGS

INGREDIENTS   Serves 4

1½ lbs. plums, pitted and
  quartered
2 tbsp. light brown sugar
1 tbsp. grated lemon rind
¼ stick butter, melted
1 tbsp. olive oil
6 sheets phyllo pastry
7 oz. orange (or lemon) curd

5 tbsp. golden raisins
confectioners' sugar,
  to decorate
low-fat plain yogurt, to serve

1 Preheat the oven to 400° F. Lightly grease an 8-inch round cake pan. Cook the plums with 2 tablespoons of the light brown sugar for 8–10 minutes to soften them, then remove from the heat and set aside.

2 Mix together the lemon rind, butter, and oil. Lay a sheet of phyllo pastry in the prepared cake pan and brush with the lemon rind mixture.

3 Cut the sheets of phyllo pastry in half and then place one half-sheet in the cake pan, and brush again.

4 Top with the remaining half-sheets of phyllo pastry, brushing each time with the lemon rind mixture. Fold each sheet in half lengthwise, to line the sides of the pan to make a phyllo shell.

5 Mix together the plums, orange curd, and golden raisins, and spoon into the phyllo pastry shell.

6 Draw the phyllo pastry edges up over the filling to enclose. Brush the remaining sheets of phyllo pastry with the lemon rind mixture and cut into thick strips.

7 Scrunch each strip of phyllo pastry and arrange on top of the pie. Cook in the preheated oven for 25 minutes until golden. Sprinkle with confectioners' sugar and serve with the plain yogurt.

HELPFUL HINT

Phyllo pastry dries out very quickly. Keep it wrapped when not using.

COFFEE & PEACH CREAMS

INGREDIENTS   Serves 4

4 peaches
¼ cup sugar
2 tbsp. coffee extract
7 oz. carton low-fat plain
  yogurt
11-oz. can reduced-fat, ready-
  made crème anglaise

TO DECORATE:
peach slices
sprigs of mint
reduced-fat sour cream

1 Cut the peaches in half and remove the pits. Place the peaches in a large bowl, cover with boiling water, and leave for 2–3 minutes.

2 Drain the peaches, then carefully remove the skin. Using a sharp knife, halve the peaches.

3 Place the sugar in a saucepan and add ¼ cup of water.

4 Bring the sugar mixture to a boil, stirring occasionally until the sugar has dissolved. Boil rapidly for about 2 minutes.

5 Add the peaches and coffee extract to the saucepan. Remove from the heat and let the peach mixture cool.

6 Meanwhile, mix together the plain yogurt and crème anglaise until well combined.

7 Divide the peach halves evenly among 4 individual glass dishes.

8 Spoon over the custard mixture, then top with the remaining peach mixture.

9 Chill in the refrigerator for 30 minutes and then serve decorated with peach slices, mint sprigs, and some sour cream.

FOOD FACT

It is generally believed that peaches originated from China. There are over 2000 varieties grown throughout the world.

SWEET-STEWED DRIED FRUITS

INGREDIENTS

Serves 4

1 lb. package mixed dried
   fruits
2 cups apple juice
2 tbsp. honey
2 tbsp. brandy
1 lemon
1 orange

TO DECORATE:
reduced-fat sour cream
fine strips of pared
   orange rind

1 Place the fruits, apple juice, honey, and brandy in a small saucepan.

2 Using a small, sharp knife or a zester, carefully remove the zest from the lemon and orange and place in the saucepan.

3 Squeeze the juice from the lemon and oranges and add to the saucepan.

4 Bring the fruit mixture to a boil, and simmer for about 1 minute. Remove the saucepan from the heat and let the mixture cool completely.

5 Transfer the mixture to a large bowl, cover with plastic wrap, and chill in the refrigerator overnight to allow the flavors to blend.

6 Spoon the stewed fruit in four shallow dessert dishes. Decorate with a large spoonful of reduced-fat sour cream and a few strips of the pared orange rind, and serve.

TASTY TIP

As a dessert, this dish is particularly good when served with cold rice pudding. However, these stewed fruits can also be very nice for breakfast. Simply pour some unsweetened granola into the bottom of a bowl, top with the stewed fruits and perhaps some low-fat plain yogurt, and serve.

TASTY TIP

Why not try for a Moroccan feel with this dish by choosing dried fruits with a selection of figs, apricots, and prunes? Add 1 teaspoon of whole cloves, a generous grating of fresh nutmeg and ginger, and 2 cinnamon sticks to the fruits in Step 1. Serve with the reduced-fat sour cream and sprinkle with a few chopped walnuts.

CHOCOLATE BRANDY DREAM

INGREDIENTS   Serves 4

6 squares low-fat chocolate,
  broken into pieces
1 cup whipping cream
2 tbsp. brandy
1 tbsp. coffee extract
1 medium egg white

TO DECORATE:
raspberries
blueberries
mint leaves
cocoa

1 Place the pieces of chocolate into a heatproof bowl placed over a saucepan of gently simmering water, and leave to slowly melt, stirring occasionally.

2 Carefully remove the saucepan and the bowl from the heat and set aside to allow the chocolate to cool.

3 Pour the cream into a small bowl, whip until soft peaks form, then set aside.

4 Gently stir the brandy and coffee extract into the chocolate. Mix together gently until blended, then fold in the whipped cream with a metal spoon or rubber spatula.

5 Briskly beat the egg white in a small bowl until stiff, then fold into the chocolate mixture with a metal spoon or rubber spatula.

6 Stir the chocolate mixture gently, taking care not to remove the air already beaten into the egg white.

7 Spoon into four tall glasses and chill in the refrigerator for at least 2 hours. Decorate with raspberries, blueberries, and mint leaves. Dust with cocoa and serve.

FOOD FACT

Careful blending is the key to recipe success in this dish, as it relies on the air beaten into both the cream and the egg whites to support the fairly heavy chocolate mixture. Take particular care when folding in the egg whites—you may find that folding just a tablespoon of the egg whites into the cream mixture may loosen the mixture, making it easier to fold in the rest of the egg whites.

FALL FRUIT LAYER

INGREDIENTS   Serves 4

1 lb. apples
2 cups blackberries
¼ cup soft brown sugar
3 tbsp. lemon juice
¼ cup low-fat spread
1¾ cups bread crumbs
2 cups nuts, chopped

red currants and mint leaves,
  to decorate
reduced-fat whipped cream or
  reduced fat ice cream,
  to serve

1 Peel, core, and slice the apples and place in a saucepan with the blackberries, sugar, and lemon juice.

2 Cover the fruit mixture and simmer, stirring occasionally, for about 15 minutes or until the apples and blackberries have formed a thick purée.

3 Remove the saucepan from the heat and allow to cool.

4 Melt the low-fat spread in a skillet and cook the bread crumbs for 5–10 minutes, stirring occasionally, until golden and crisp.

5 Remove the skillet from the heat and stir in the nuts. Allow to cool.

6 Alternately layer the fruit purée and bread crumbs into four tall glasses.

7 Store the desserts in the refrigerator to chill, and remove when ready to serve.

8 Decorate with red currants and mint leaves, and serve with reduced-fat whipped cream or reduced fat vanilla or raspberry ice cream.

TASTY TIP

Any fall fruit can be used in this recipe. Add pears to this recipe to make an apple and pear fruit layer, or use some plums if preferred. For a more textured dessert, reduce the amount of bread crumbs used to 1 cup and add ⅔ cup of rolled oats in Step 5.

FRUIT & OAT PUDDINGS

INGREDIENTS   Serves 4

1¼ cups rolled oats
¼ cup low-fat spread, melted
2 tbsp. chopped almonds
1 tbsp. honey
pinch of ground cinnamon
2 pears, peeled, cored, and
  finely chopped
1 tbsp. marmalade

orange zest, to decorate
low-fat custard or fruit-
  flavored low-fat yogurt,
  to serve

1 Preheat the oven to 400° F. Lightly grease and line the bases of 4 individual ovenproof bowls or muffin pans with a small circle of waxed paper.

2 Mix together the oats, low-fat spread, nuts, honey, and cinnamon in a small bowl.

3 Using a spoon, spread two thirds of the mixture over the base and around the sides of the ovenproof bowls or muffin pans.

4 Toss together the pears and marmalade, and spoon into the oat shells.

5 Sprinkle with the remaining oat mixture to cover the pears and marmalade.

6 Cook in the preheated oven for 15–20 minutes until cooked and the tops of the desserts are golden and crisp.

7 Leave for 5 minutes before removing the ovenproof bowls or the muffin pans. Decorate with orange zest and serve hot with low-fat custard or yogurt.

TASTY TIP

Liqueured crème anglaise is great with steamed desserts. Add 2–3 tablespoons of a liqueur of your choice to the crème anglaise, along with 1 teaspoon of vanilla extract. Taste, and add more liquer if desired.

FRUIT SALAD

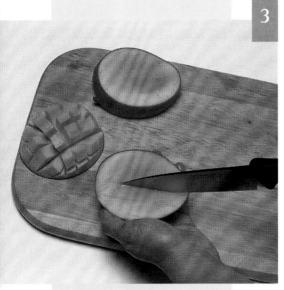

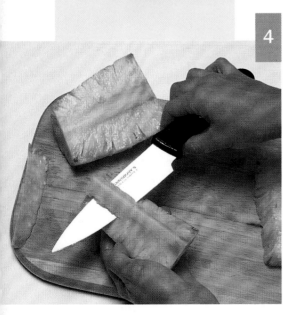

INGREDIENTS   Serves 4

½ cup sugar
3 oranges
2 14-oz. cans lychees
1 small mango
1 small pineapple
1 papaya
4 pieces stem ginger, in syrup
4 tbsp. stem ginger syrup
¾ cup cherries

1 cup strawberries, hulled
½ tsp. almond extract

TO DECORATE:
mint leaves
lime zest

1. Place the sugar and 1¼ cups of water in a small saucepan and heat, gently stirring until the sugar has dissolved. Bring to a boil and simmer for 2 minutes. Once a syrup has formed, remove from the heat and allow to cool.

2. Using a sharp knife, cut away the skin from the oranges, then slice thickly. Cut each slice in half and place in a serving dish with the syrup and lychees.

3. Peel the mango, then cut into thick slices around each side of the pit. Discard the pit and cut the slices into bite-size pieces and add to the syrup.

4. Using a sharp knife again, carefully cut away the skin from the pineapple.

5. Remove the central core using the knife or an apple corer, then cut the pineapple into segments and add to the syrup.

6. Peel the papaya, then cut in half and remove the seeds. Cut the flesh into chunks, slice the ginger into matchsticks, and add with the ginger syrup to the fruit in the syrup.

7. Halve the strawberries, add to the fruit with the cherries and almond extract, and chill in the refrigerator for 30 minutes. Sprinkle with mint leaves and lime zest to decorate, and serve.

FOOD FACT

Lychees are native to China. If they are unavailable, try using grapes as a substitute.

SUMMER PAVLOVA

INGREDIENTS   Serves 6–8

4 medium egg whites
1 cup sugar
1 tsp. vanilla extract
2 tsp. white wine vinegar
1½ tsp. cornstarch
1 cup low-fat plain yogurt
2 tbsp. honey

2 cups strawberries, hulled
1 cup raspberries
1 cup blueberries
4 kiwis, peeled and sliced
confectioners' sugar,
  to decorate

1 Preheat the oven to 300° F. Line a baking sheet with a sheet of waxed paper or baking parchment.

2 Place the egg whites in a clean, grease-free bowl and beat until very stiff.

3 Beat in half the sugar, the vanilla extract, vinegar, and cornstarch, and continue beating until stiff.

4 Gradually, beat in the remaining sugar, a teaspoonful at a time, until very stiff and glossy.

5 Using a large spoon, arrange spoonfuls of the meringue in a circle on the waxed paper or baking parchment.

6 Cook the meringue in the preheated oven for 1 hour or until crisp and dry. Turn the oven off and leave the meringue in the oven to allow it to cool completely.

7 Remove the meringue from the baking sheet and peel away the baking parchment. Mix together the yogurt and honey. Place the pavlova on a serving plate and spoon the yogurt into the center.

8 Sprinkle with the strawberries, raspberries, blueberries, and kiwis. Dust with the confectioners' sugar and serve.

HELPFUL HINT

Always remember to double-check that the bowl being used to beat egg whites is completely clean, as you will find that any grease will prevent the egg whites from rising into the stiff consistency necessary for this recipe.

POACHED PEARS

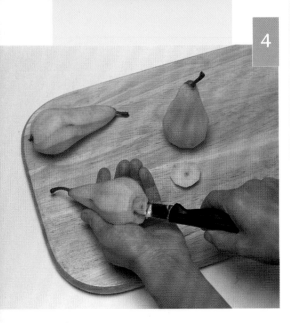

INGREDIENTS

Serves 4

2 small cinnamon sticks
½ cup sugar
1¼ cups red wine
⅔ cup water
1 tbsp. thinly pared orange
   rind
1 tbsp. orange juice

4 firm pears
orange slices, to decorate
frozen vanilla yogurt or
   low-fat ice cream, to serve

1 Place the cinnamon sticks on the clean work surface, and with a rolling pin, slowly roll down the side of the cinnamon stick to bruise. Place in a large, heavy saucepan.

2 Add the sugar, wine, water, pared orange rind, and juice to the saucepan, and bring slowly to a boil, stirring occasionally until the sugar has dissolved.

3 Meanwhile, peel the pears, leaving the stalks on.

4 Cut out the cores from the bottoms of the pears, and level them so that they stand upright.

5 Stand the pears in the syrup, cover the saucepan, and simmer for 20 minutes or until tender.

6 Remove the saucepan from the heat and let the pears cool in the syrup, turning them occasionally.

7 Arrange the pears on serving plates and spoon over the syrup. Decorate with the orange slices and serve with the yogurt or low-fat ice cream and any remaining juices.

TASTY TIP

Poached pears are delicious served with a little reduced-fat sour cream and sprinkled with toasted almonds. To toast almonds, simply warm the broiler and place whole, blanched almonds or slivered almonds onto a piece of foil. Place under the broiler and toast lightly on both sides for 1–2 minutes until golden. Remove and cool; chop if desired.

GRAPE & ALMOND LAYER

INGREDIENTS   Serves 4

1 cup reduced-fat sour cream
1 cup low-fat plain yogurt
3 tbsp. confectioners' sugar,
   sifted
2 tbsp. crème de cassis
1 lb. red grapes
2 cups Amaretto cookies

2 ripe passion fruit

TO DECORATE:
confectioners' sugar
extra grapes (optional)

1 Mix together the sour cream and yogurt in a bowl, and lightly fold in the sifted confectioners' sugar and the crème de cassis with a large metal spoon or rubber spatula until lightly blended.

2 Using a small knife, remove the seeds from the grapes, if necessary. Rinse lightly and pat dry on absorbent paper towels.

3 Place the seeded grapes in a bowl and stir in any juice from the grapes left over from seeding.

4 Place the Amaretto cookies in a plastic bag and crush coarsely with a rolling pin. Alternatively, use a food processor.

5 Cut the passion fruit in half, scoop out the seeds with a teaspoon, and set aside.

6 Divide the yogurt mixture among 4 tall glasses, then layer alternately with grapes, crushed cookies, and most of the passion fruit seeds. Top with the yogurt mixture and the remaining passion fruit seeds. Chill in the refrigerator for 1 hour and decorate with extra grapes. Lightly dust with confectioners' sugar and serve.

FOOD FACT

Passion fruit is native to Brazil. They are purple in color and are about the size of an egg. Look for fruits that are wrinkled, not smooth. When wrinkled, they are ripe and at their best.

SUMMER PUDDING

INGREDIENTS   Serves 4

4 cups red currants
½ cup sugar
3 cups strawberries, hulled
  and halved
1 cup raspberries
2 tbsp. Grand Marnier
  or Cointreau
8–10 medium slices white
  bread, crusts removed
mint sprigs, to decorate

low-fat plain yogurt or
reduced-fat sour cream,
to serve

1 Place the red currants, sugar, and 1 tablespoon of water in a large saucepan. Heat gently until the sugar has just dissolved and the juices have just begun to run.

2 Remove the saucepan from the heat and stir in the strawberries, raspberries, and the Grand Marnier or Cointreau.

3 Line the base and sides of a 1-quart ovenproof bowl with two thirds of the bread, making sure that the slices overlap each other slightly.

4 Spoon the fruit with their juices into the bread-lined ovenproof bowl, then top with the remaining bread slices.

5 Place a small plate on top of the dessert inside the ovenproof bowl. Ensure the plate fits tightly, then weigh down with a clean can or some weights, and chill in the refrigerator overnight.

6 When ready to serve, remove the weights and plate. Carefully loosen around the sides of the basin with a round-bladed knife. Invert the dessert onto a serving plate, decorate with the mint sprigs, and serve with the yogurt or sour cream.

TASTY TIP

This really is a summer dessert, using plump, juicy berries that are bursting with flavor. Why not try a fall version using seasonal fruit such as blackberries, plums, and flavorful apples? Place in just a few tablespoons of water, along with ¼ cup of sugar, and heat gently as in Step 1.

CARAMELIZED ORANGES IN AN ICED BOWL

INGREDIENTS

Serves 4

FOR THE ICE BOWL:
about 36 ice cubes
fresh flowers and fruits
8 medium oranges

1 cup sugar
4 tbsp. Grand Marnier
  or Cointreau

1 Place a few ice cubes in the base of a 2-quart freezable glass bowl. Place a 1-quart glass bowl on top of the ice cubes. Arrange the flowerheads and fruits between the 2 bowls, wedging in position with the ice cubes.

2 Weigh down the smaller bowl with some heavy weights, then carefully pour cold water between the 2 bowls, making sure that the flowers and the fruit are covered. Freeze for at least 6 hours or until the ice is frozen solid.

3 When ready to use, remove the weights, and using a hot, damp cloth, rub the inside of the smaller bowl with the cloth until it loosens sufficiently for you to remove the bowl. Place the larger bowl in the sink, half-filled with hot water. Leave for 30 seconds or until the ice loosens. Take care not to leave the bowl in the water for too long, otherwise the ice will melt. Remove the bowl from the sink and leave in the refrigerator. Return the freezer to its normal setting.

4 Thinly pare the rind from 2 oranges and then julienne. Using a sharp knife, cut away the rind and pith from all the oranges, holding over a bowl to catch the juices. Slice the oranges, discarding any seeds, and re-form each orange back to its original shape. Secure with toothpicks, then place in a bowl.

5 Heat 1¼ cups water, the orange rind, and sugar together in a saucepan. Stir the sugar until dissolved. Bring to a boil. Boil for 15 minutes until it is a caramel color. Remove from the heat.

6 Stir in the liqueur, then add the oranges. Allow to cool. Chill for 3 hours, turning the oranges occasionally. Spoon into the ice bowl and serve.

HELPFUL HINT

This ice bowl can hold any dessert. Why not fill it with flavored ice creams?

RASPBERRY SORBET CRUSH

INGREDIENTS   Serves 4

2 cups raspberries
2 tsp. grated lime rind
1 tbsp. lime juice

1¼ cups orange juice
1 cup sugar
2 medium egg whites

1 Pick over the raspberries and lightly rinse under cold running water.

2 Place the raspberries in a dish and, using a masher, mash to a chunky purée.

3 Place the lime rind and juice, orange juice, and half the sugar in a large, heavy saucepan.

4 Heat gently, stirring frequently, until the sugar has dissolved. Bring to a boil, and boil rapidly for about 5 minutes.

5 Remove the saucepan from the heat and pour carefully into a freezable container.

6 Allow to cool, then place in the freezer and freeze for 2 hours, stirring occasionally to break up the ice crystals.

7 Fold the ice mixture into the raspberry purée and freeze for an additional 2 hours, stirring occasionally.

8 Beat the egg whites until stiff, then gradually beat in the remaining sugar, a tablespoon at a time, until the egg white mixture is stiff and glossy.

9 Fold into the raspberry sorbet with a metal spoon and freeze for 1 hour. Spoon into tall glasses and serve immediately.

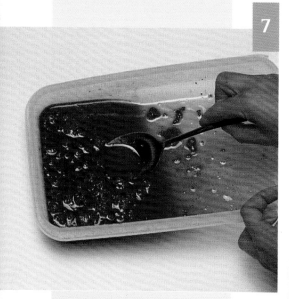

FOOD FACT

This recipe contains raw egg, and should not be given to babies, young children, pregnant women, the sick, the elderly, and those with a compromised immune system.

RASPBERRY SOUFFLÉ

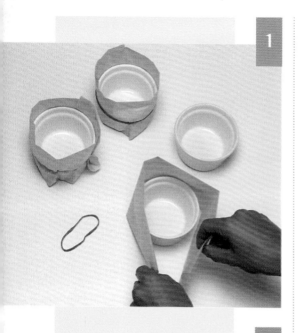

INGREDIENTS

Serves 4

1 cup red currants
¼ cup sugar
3 tsp. powdered gelatin
3 medium eggs, separated
1 cup low-fat plain yogurt
4 cups raspberries, defrosted
  if frozen

TO DECORATE:

mint sprigs
extra fruits

1 Wrap a band of double-thickness waxed paper around 4 ramekin dishes, making sure that 2 inches of the paper stay above the top of each dish. Secure the paper to the dish with an elastic band or adhesive tape.

2 Place the red currants and 1 tablespoon of the sugar in a saucepan. Cook for 5 minutes until softened. Remove from the heat, strain, and set aside.

3 Place 3 tablespoons of water in a small bowl and sprinkle over the gelatin. Let stand for 5 minutes until spongy. Place the bowl over a saucepan of simmering water and leave until dissolved. Remove and let cool.

4 Beat together the remaining sugar and egg yolks until pale, thick, and creamy, then fold in the plain yogurt with a large metal spoon or rubber spatula until well blended.

5 Strain the raspberries and fold into the yogurt mixture with the gelatin. Beat the egg whites until stiff, and fold into the yogurt mixture. Pour into the prepared dishes and chill in the refrigerator for 2 hours until firm.

6 Remove the paper from the dishes and spread the red currant purée over the top of the soufflés. Decorate with mint sprigs and extra fruits, and serve.

HELPFUL HINT

Soufflés rely on air, so it is important that the egg whites in this recipe are beaten until very stiff in order to support the other mixture.

FRUITY ROULADE

INGREDIENTS
Serves 4

FOR THE SPONGE:
3 medium eggs
½ cup sugar
¾ cup all-purpose flour, sifted
1–2 tbsp. sugar, for sprinkling

FOR THE FILLING:
½ cup quark
½ cup low-fat plain yogurt
2 tbsp. sugar

1 tbsp. orange liqueur
(optional)
1 tbsp. grated orange rind
1 cup strawberries, hulled and
cut into quarters

TO DECORATE:
strawberries
sifted confectioners' sugar

1 Preheat the oven to 425° F.
Lightly grease and line a 9 x
13 inch jelly-roll pan with baking
parchment.

2 Using an electric whisk, beat
the eggs and sugar until the
mixture has doubled in volume
and leaves a trail across the top.

3 Fold in the flour with a metal
spoon or rubber spatula.
Pour into the prepared pan and
cook in the preheated oven for
10–12 minutes until well risen
and golden.

4 Place a whole sheet of
baking parchment out on a
clean, flat work surface and
sprinkle evenly with the sugar.

5 Turn the cooked sponge out
onto the paper, discard the
paper, trim the sponge, and roll
up, encasing the paper inside.
Set aside until cool.

6 To make the filling, mix
together the quark, yogurt,
sugar, liqueur (if using), and
orange rind. Unroll the roulade
and spread over the mixture.
Sprinkle with the strawberries
and roll up.

7 Decorate the roulade with
strawberries. Dust with the
confectioners' sugar and serve.

FOOD FACT

Quark is a soft, unripened
cheese with the flavor and
texture of sour cream. It
comes in two varieties, low-
fat and nonfat. It can be used
as a sour cream substitute to
top baked potatoes or in dips
and cheesecakes.

INDEX